Craft your dest

Aha! Moment
J O U R N A L

Jae M. Rang

Published by
Hasmark Publishing, judy@hasmarkservices.com
Copyright © 2017 Jae M. Rang www.ahamoments.ca
First Edition, 2017

Disclaimer

Permission should be addressed in writing to Jae M. Rang at
jae@jaeassociates.com

Cover Design by Patti Knoles
Patti.knoles@gmail.com

Design & Layout by Anne Karklins
annekarklins@gmail.com

ISBN-13: 978-1-988071-80-0
ISBN-10: 1988071801

This book is dedicated to you and
your profound happiness.
Live from the heart. Be a best friend.
Enjoy every moment.

What people are saying about the
AHA! MOMENT JOURNAL

"*Have you ever had a mental epiphany that completely changed your perspective, and opened up a whole new way of thinking? They are normally pretty rare, but I'm sure you remember just how impactful that 'Aha Moment' was in transforming your thinking, and your subsequent results. This genius journal is flooded with lessons that will trigger break-throughs, shift your perspective, and inevitably improve your life.*"

~ William Mahood, Founder VRSN, Nutrition Coach, Oakville, Ontario, Canada

"*This* Aha! Journal *brings together 2 amazing concepts that will be personally transformative. First are the amazing stories that showcase a significant and interesting point of view. I am familiar with them over the years and these have often changed or reinforced a paradigm shift for me. Adding the ability to journal about these stories using a question as a starting point, will help to clarify your thinking on these subjects. I believe that this new* Aha! Journal *is the best of both worlds and will help anyone continue to grow and learn in a positive direction. Thank you Jae for this fantastic* Aha! Journal!"

~ Jennifer L. Murdoch B.A. (Hons) ACII, AIC, Insurance Professional, Bermuda

"*Jae M. Rang has compiled a remarkable book filled with inspiration and original, practical advice for making the most of our lives and the talents we've all been given. It's a refreshing read that reminds me to occasionally stop, take a deep breath and really consider what matters. Thinking like this can change your life.*"

~ Tina Berres Filipski, PPAI, Director of Publications/Editor, Irving, Texas, USA

"*Anyone wishing to grow to their potential knows the value of thinking outside the box. This journal facilitates just that in an incredibly unique way that brings positive change easily. Held captive by relatable stories, you'll find yourself focused and inspired with the turn of each page. Everyone deserves a copy of this book!*"

~ Emma O'Dwyer, BAH, MBA, GEMBA, Toronto, Ontario, Canada

"Jae brilliantly merged the quaint idea of hand writing with the latest brain science in the Aha! Moment Journal. *Since it's all about you, the outcome is always tailored to you. The* Aha! Moment Journal *provides a simple yet sophisticated way to access your genius to lead a life uniquely suited to your fulfillment. If you engage consistently in Jae's easy to use process, your results will speak for themselves. Simple. Sophisticated. Powerful.*"

~ Ann Elliott, founder of The Berkana Company, a business consulting and executive coaching company. Columbia, South Carolina, USA

"*The* Aha! Moment Journal *is an inspiring collection of short stories that provide "aha" moments for the reader; very uplifting and enjoyable to read. Will make a lovely gift for someone, too.*"

~ Paulette Vinette, CAE, FASAE, President, Solution Studio Inc., Oakville, Ontario, Canada

"*If you want to change the results in your life, but don't know where to start, pick up the* Aha! Journal. *You will lead yourself on a journey of self-discovery where many answers will appear, but only when you give your brain this break. As you work through this journal, you will experience flashes of insight, solve life's challenges, and progress in ways that are beyond your imagination. If you want to take your results to the next level, begin working with the* Aha! Journal *today.*"

~ Andrea Samadi, author of *Level Up: A Brain-Based Strategy to Skyrocket Student Success and Achievement* and founder of www.achieveit360.com , California, USA

"*Every Monday morning, rain or shine, I have looked forward to Jae's* Aha! Moment *appearing in my Inbox! Often, being deeply touched by the message, I have forwarded these 'little gems' to co-workers and family members across the country! Brilliantly, Jae has now compiled her short* Aha! Moment *reflections into a Journal designed to encourage her readers to explore their ability to contemplate and record how a particular inspiration might be implemented to enhance their own lives. This Journal will be a gift to those who desire to grow personally as well as professionally!*"

~ Jean Ann Ronci, Partner, Faro Products Inc., Montreal, Quebec, Canada

"*Who hasn't had a moment when they need a reminder of something they subconsciously know? The* Aha! Moment Journal *gives you the wisdom you need when you need it and anchors it even deeper with its handy action plan right so that you can record your own moments to refer back to when the challenge rears its mischievous head. Great little journal to keep handy.*"

~ Kaz Lefave, author of *Nemecene*, Toronto, Ontario, Canada

"*The* Aha! Moment Journal *is an amazing tool that nudges a person to gain a clear perspective of what success means to them, along with identifying who, what, where and how it can all come together. It contains a beautiful blend of self-reflection, clarity of goals by pursuing solid business and personal development practices to assist in the journey of achieving their desired success. A great tool to use personally, as well as a great gift!*"

~ Linda McLean, CEO & Founder, McLean International, Speaker, Author, Coach, Nevada, USA

"*Having subscribed to the* Aha! Moments *Newsletter for years now, I already knew what a unique and smart style Jae M. Rang had of presenting ideas and sparking deeper thought for its readers! With The* Aha! Moments Journal, *Jae has provided a thought provoking medium with which to connect to our own inner truths and spark beautiful insights that will expand the world within which we are currently living. I can't recommend this journal enough, it is a gift to your creative self that will not only engage new ways of thinking but will connect you to your inner wisdom and bring forward a positive shift to your entire life!*"

~ Cathy Chmilnitzky, Energy Intuitive, Teacher, Author and Owner of Energy Mastery Institute, Caledon, Ontario, Canada

"*Jae's* Aha! Moments *are truly inspiring insights that I look forward to receiving each week. Her Aha's are a testament to the truth that big change can be achieved through little, consistent adjustments and shifts in thinking. Having been a constant consumer of Jae's inspirations, I know embracing the compilation of the Aha's set out in this journal will create game-changing results for anyone who intends to meaningfully shift their life circumstances for the better.*"

~ Laura K. Williams, Principal, Williams HR Law Professional Corporation, Toronto Ontario, Canada

"I simply love Jae M. Rang's Aha! Moment Journal. *It is a gift for anyone wanting to have moments of inspiration and wisdom. This journal is insightful and practical. I believe everyone should have one and give one away as a gift to someone they deeply care about."*

~ Peggy McColl, New York Times Best Selling Author, Ottawa, Ontario, Canada

"I've loved seeing the Aha! Moments *pop into my email on Monday mornings. No matter how busy the start of the week, Jae's inspirational quotes help to kick start my week and set positive intentions for the week ahead. Many times, I've forwarded them onto my family and friends to instill Jae's insight and enthusiasm into them! This journal is surely the icing on the cake for everyone wishing to advance by shaking up their thinking. Thanks Jae for pulling this collection of Aha's together in a way that will help anyone grow!"*

~ Marty Britton, President, Britton Management Profiles Inc., Toronto, Ontario, Canada

"Jae's Aha! Moments *are reminders to reset and consider what adventure lies ahead that is just begging to be written. Understand that sometimes we get what we need instead of what we think we want; however, in each moment there is always something to be learned and appreciated. Each Aha! invites some contemplation time to create what might be."*

~ Barbara Dobreen, Elected Official/Councillor, Township of Southgate, Ontario, Canada

"I have benefited from the wisdom and humor in Aha! Moment *Monday for several years. Now, Jae has taken it to the next level with* Aha! Moment Journal. *The journal encourages me to consider the application of Jae's insights to my own life through thoughtful questioning and journaling exercises. I recommend* Aha! Moment Journal *for anyone who is on the quest to improve their life!"*

~ Kathy Petrowsky Ph.D, Garnett, Kansas, USA

"When I first started receiving the Aha! Moment *Mondays, I was reading them to support a friend. As the weeks went by I found myself looking forward to seeing what insights Jae had for me. After few more times I realized how much I related to the stories. The amazing part of* Aha! Moments *is that they started shaping my mornings and my day*

to follow. I was finding there was something that I could take with me wherever I went whether it was a client meeting, board meeting or even when I was on the golf course enjoying the game I love so much. My subconscious mind was working and bringing me the best results. Talk about power! Every moment is an important moment but sharing Aha! Moments is sharing the love and passion you feel for others."

~ Asha Singh, Realtor, Royal Le Page Signature Reality, Mississauga, Ontario, Canada

"What a wonderful idea! I simply could not stop reading and actually writing responses. Some days it was hard to stop at just one. I love the idea of writing so much that I even use a program on my iPad that allows me to write as though on a notepad. I love the idea of the Aha! Journal to be able to return to areas and see what I thought before and see how I've grown. Please, even if it's only a line or two, start this and let it help you grow. You'll create an additional page to thank yourself for doing so!"

~ Carolyn Morse, President, PowerLung Inc., Houston, Texas, USA

"Jae, I have found your Aha's so wonderfully insightful and inspiring; but of course that is to be expected from someone as focused, dedicated and thoughtful as you. I am sure the book will be a great success and very helpful to all who take the time to read it."

~ Laura Boyd-Brown

"A hearty Aha! to this gem of a journaling tool. I'm a firm believer both that what we think about we bring about, and also that writing those thoughts is far more powerful than typing them. Thank you for putting together such an accessible tool to keep me thinking and growing. I'll be gifting this to several friends and clients!"

~ Amy Stoehr, President and Executive Coach, McLean International, Boulder, Colorado, USA

"*Life's events are unfolding in a continuous way and we get life's valuable lessons if, and only if, we are aware how it is evolving. This* Aha! Moment Journal *is an essential tool to use for your awakening because it is rich of insightful messages that will take you from one Aha! moment to the other!*"

~ Dr. Jussi Eerikäinen, Cardiologist & Mathematician, International Bestselling Author of *Transforming Vibes, Transforming Lives*, Tenerife, the Canary Islands, Spain

"*Jae M. Rang's* Aha! Moment Journal *takes the reader on a journey of self discovery to understand their thinking through powerful storytelling and thought provoking statements. Masterful work. A must for all.*"

~ Chari Schwartz, Certified Coach Frame of Mind Coaching, Toronto, Ontario, Canada

FOREWORD

Everyone has a gift. Perhaps yours is in organization or leadership. Maybe you've chosen a field because of your level of compassion or ability to engineer or teach or sprint or protect. Me? I'm an artist at the core.

My earliest passion was in the performing arts which started when I was three years old. Since then I've been honored to portray a vast range of characters in over 20 films and eight television series; one of which allowed me the privilege of a role in the pop culture sensation, *Melrose Place*.

Having graduated from USM's Masters Program in Spiritual Psychology, I understand the significance of focusing on what you want, as opposed to what you don't want. That spirit of curiosity and desire for me to bring as much joy to as many people as I am able sparked a second channel of creativity in the culinary arts and then another as an entrepreneur.

Life is unfolding one little moment at a time, and it's in those little moments that life's lessons occur. In fact school is always in session.

But the lessons don't appear when you're living unconsciously. I've discovered that by being open and vulnerable and allowing myself to entertain new ways of thinking, I achieve breakthroughs. Being open to shift perspective – to look at something simple or routine with a hint of newness – brings life's finest rewards.

As creatures of habit, shifting perspective is not routine so we need to be intentional.

You know, for years I've witnessed writers agonize over the perfect script. That helped me realize the importance of words; the words we say out loud and the ones we say to ourselves. The ones we read and write and allow that describe our lives and those in it. You are what you say and with what you surround yourself. I've taken to investing in quiet time and journaling, experiencing that together they are exceptional ways to get in touch with my authentic self, to explore my perspective and the words I choose to use and share.

This *Aha! Moment Journal* is an essential tool for everyone looking to advance themselves and I'm ecstatic that my friend Jae, who speaks the same inspired language as I do, has pulled these insightful messages together in a way that enables thinking, empathy, engagement and growth. Each Aha! is a real life moment with an easily accessible yet truly profound perspective shift that makes the path to enlightenment available. To get the most out of this handbook, open up a page then give yourself the gift of a few minutes to ponder the message, journal the actions then take being "you" to a whole new level.

I believe we all have all the answers we need right inside of us, but sometimes we need a spark. The *Aha! Moment Journal* is that spark.

Jamie Luner, Actor, Entrepreneur

INTRODUCTION

"When you change the way you look at things,
the things you look at change."

~ Wayne Dyer

Welcome!

I'm looking so forward to going on this journey with you.

I say, "with you" because in this journal you'll get a glimpse into some of the [greater] life-changing situations and experiences I've had the past few years as a business professional, a teacher, a student and a mom. (I think you'll relate to most of them.) You'll see the shifts in perspective that MADE each one so life-changing. AND...

You'll discover how to create such "turning points" in your own life, almost at will. You see, this book is not just about sharing. It's a tool to create real breakthroughs... YOUR breakthroughs.

The "Aha!" stories themselves are written to elicit different "lessons" or "realizations" in different people. Or to put it another way, there is no "one right way" to interpret any given story, and you're free to draw whatever conclusion, and whatever lesson, makes sense FOR YOU!

This is by design... because I've found this is the BEST way to change habits (and paradigms). When the lesson wells up from deep within YOU, rather than being shoved down your throat by someone else, any resulting change is more meaningful and long-lasting.

Now, it's a funny thing about paradigms. They control about 95% of everything we do... but we understand so very little about them.

Allow me to explain.

Ninety-five percent of everything we do is automatic. The way we comb our hair, put on our pants, get ready to drive out of the driveway, introduce ourselves to another, smile, walk, eat, sleep, speak, parent, pray, invest, organize ourselves – almost everything – is done on auto pilot. We almost never think. We think we think, but in fact we don't... most of the time.

As Bob Proctor, author of *You Were Born Rich*, explains, "A paradigm is an emotionally fixed idea."

A paradigm is a perspective that results from conditioning. And your conditioning is simply the neurons in your brain making connections and creating pathways to remember how you did something, or how you thought, or were taught to think about something, the first time. That way it's easier to do it the next time, and the next, and the next… the more you perform that task or apply that perspective, the more fixed that action or perspective becomes.

Habits are nature's way of protecting us from getting overwhelmed with constant details. Could you imagine if every time you brushed your teeth you had to think through the process? Where is my tooth-brush? How do I hold it? What's my cleaning sequence? Learning routine tasks over and over would be exhausting so we're wired for habits. "Doing" in a certain way, and more importantly, "acting" in a certain way becomes routinely comfortable. We can't say "thinking" in a certain way because being on auto-pilot isn't really thinking.

Paradigms begin to take shape long before our conscious mind is aware of what's happening. We become a product of our environment – those who care for us and teach us become our greatest influence – which means many of our choices and our perspectives are the result of years of programming.

Now here's the incredible part:

Listen to this: Recent studies show that our paradigms can be traced back as far as SIX GENERATIONS through our DNA!

So we are who we are but we don't necessarily know how we got that way. We can look at our parents and grandparents, aunts and uncles, teachers and caregivers for some answers, but suffice to say that we chose very little of it.

While much of our conditioning is in place by the time we're six years of age, the balance is often acquired through our senses: sight, hearing, smell, taste, and touch. That which we experience through our senses shapes our opinions, our actions and our reactions.

It also shapes our results.

For years we believed that once we were wired, we were wired – that those neuropathways were irreversible and there was no chance of changing who we are. New research in neuroplasticity proves that we

CAN rewire our brains, that we CAN change our paradigms, and that we CAN develop new habits and perspectives that serve us better.

So that's the science behind what you're about to experience as you play your way through the Aha! Journal! The thing is, all that science-y stuff is going to happen whether you're AWARE of it or not! So I don't want you to get hung up on it, if it didn't quite "click" with you.

Just have FUN with what's ahead… and all that stuff will happen for you without even thinking about it.

Deep down we all desire to live a fulfilling life – to love and be loved and to live with purpose and meaning. It's inherent in our nature to want to matter. Sometimes our conditioning sabotages that desire – and we believe, for a variety of reasons, that we cannot attain, or don't deserve, joy and success.

While we might be 95% programmed, we have the ability to change that programming – to change our view, change our habits, change our belief – by changing our perspective. We can CHOOSE a life of abundance many only imagine is possible.

In the late 90's I had the pleasure of meeting and working with Bob Proctor, the famed philosopher in, "The Secret". To this day Bob and I remain closely connected and I've had the good fortune to expand my network of teachers – researchers and practitioners – allowing me to totally indulge in the study and sharing of universal principals, human behaviour and neuroplasticity. Not only has the investment in these areas been of significance in my marketing practice, it's totally shaped my life. You see it's when you purposely choose to take responsibility for your life that life rewards you.

This *Aha! Moment Journal* is all about choosing to expand. It's all about choosing to put your auto-pilot on hold and rather than judge through your programmed filters, to allow yourself to imagine.

You see, imagination shuts off the senses – the place where our programming is typically initiated –and allows you to do some original thinking. And while you may be compelled to shift your thinking by simply *reading* an Aha, the REAL CHANGE occurs when you journal. Because writing causes thinking.

There is a Chinese proverb that goes like this: "Tell me and I'll forget; show me and I may remember; involve me and I'll understand."

Open to the first Aha! or to any page you're drawn to. The Ahas aren't written in any particular order and there is no sequence or frequency by which you should read them. Follow your intuition and inspiration. Read the Aha, digest the question, journal your response and entertain a new perspective.

Now, notice that the "Action" items you'll be journaling are often in the form of questions. That's done deliberately.

Dr Jussi Eerikainen, author of *Transforming Vibes, Transforming Lives* says, "When you ask a question of your mind, it immediately begins to work on finding the answer to that question or to solve the problem. Questions are far more powerful than affirmations alone."

Interesting, eh? (Aha! My "Canadian" is showing)

Because we're programmed to think from the outside in (we now know that's not "thinking", it's "responding") we often impose unfair and limiting beliefs on ourselves and our ability.

Dr. Jussi points out a big flaw in that way of shaping ourselves. "When you watch the news every single day, you end up having a negative mindset, which is just going to make you feel the world is collapsing entirely. If that were the case, why would you ever want to work, study, invest, form a family and so forth? But, if we truly measure what we have, and we must delve more into that issue, the world is becoming exceptionally better."

We're the highest form of creation on this planet with endless capability! The problem is, it's not who you are that holds you back, it's who you think you're not.

Understand that belief is based on your evaluation of something. When your evaluation changes, so does your belief.

It's thinking that promotes real growth – imagination and original thought – and you'll jump-start that into high gear simply by journaling your responses page by page.

And at anytime on your journey, connect with us at www.ahamoments.ca to learn more, share more, and have more.

Enjoy your journey.

Be willing to be surprised.

Know you always end up in the perfect place… for you.

Now let's get started!

Jae M. Rang

Strategist, Speaker, Author, Mom

How is your penmanship?

Is it clear, structured and consistent or is it creative, loopy and… well, people say that you should have been a doctor?

I'm w-a-y faster, clearer and more accurate with a keyboard than with a pen. Even I have trouble reading my writing sometimes.

Now the flat screen is a whole other ball game.

I watch people zip through messages with two thumbs blazing and I'm wowed with their accuracy. (I think I spend as much time correcting my prose than writing it in the first place.)

Handwriting analysts can tell a lot about an individual's character by their handwriting. Perhaps analyzing is as much of a lost art as cursive itself because when we keyboard, all of our writing looks the same.

Sure we can choose our font, emojis and how many exclamation marks we add to make a point but essentially, electronic communication has imposed structure… like the lines in a colouring book.

By losing our interest in cursive, are we inhibiting our creativity?

In a study by Virginia Berninger, a professor at the University of Washington, she reveals children in grades two, four and six wrote more words faster and expressed more ideas when writing their essays by hand as opposed to with a keyboard.

Aha! – We're most in touch with our creative centre with pen in hand.

Writing causes thinking.

In an article in *Psychology Today*, Dr. William R. Klemm writes, "…In the case of learning cursive writing, the brain develops functional specialization that integrates both sensation, movement control and thinking. Cursive writing trains the brain to integrate visual and tactile information and fine motor dexterity."

When you write, you actually have to pay attention and think and areas of the brain are activated that are not so during typing. And it turns out, the more meaningful the context, the more activation there is in both hemispheres of the brain.

The keyboard is perfect for transcribing, documenting and sharing what we already know. But when you want to max your pure potential, your favourite writing instrument is your creativity's best friend.

Write on!

Action: Spend a moment writing out your ideal day in detail. Who are you with? What are you doing?

Have you ever had something not turn out the way you expected it?

You envision the outcome, prepare the work, rehearse the dialogue, give it your best shot with all the light beams in the world behind you and... ugh... the outcome falls short of your expectation.

So you shake your head, look for the lesson, and then what?

We all know that failure is simply a stepping stone to success.

(One mentor of mine used to say, "If you want to succeed faster, fail faster.")

But how does the conversation sound; the one that runs through your head after you've dusted yourself off and are ready for the next go 'round?

Is the level of anxiety, fear of failure or self-judgment, cranked up a notch?

Seth Godin calls it, "invented suffering" and observes, "...when we do contribute, having experienced so much in our internal narrative, our instinct is to demand gratitude ... and prizes ... and an end to the suffering we've created."

Often we're our own worse critics and our need for a softer landing increases to offset the torture we put ourselves through ahead of time!

Aha! – End the suffering by shifting expectations.

There is a difference between taking responsibility for your actions and taking responsibility for the outcome. You're not in complete control of the outcome – ever – you can only influence it.

Even when you're absolutely positively sure you've anticipated every possible hurdle and prepared for any outcome, life is dynamic. The only control you have is with your expectation, your effort, and how you respond to the outcome.

The gratitude, in response to your efforts, might appear to close the gap, complete the circle and make you feel that what you gave was needed.

Regardless of how the outcome appears, your efforts are always needed.

The world needs you, "...to do it again, to care again and to seek to make change, again."

Keep going!!

Action: Identify a goal to which you are so attached that the hurdles are causing grief. What one expectation can you change to allow the outcome to materialize without force?

_____

_____

_____

_____

_____

_____

_____

_____

_____

_____

_____

_____

_____

_____

_____

_____

_____

_____

_____

There's nothing more fun than having fun!

Now the definition of "fun" is different for different people, but one thing we all have in common is that we love to laugh.

When we say it "feels good to laugh" we're not kidding.

Laughter not only lifts us emotionally but because laughter is proven to decrease stress hormones and increased immune cells and infection-fighting antibodies, it really does feel good to laugh!

Laughter keeps our bodies at ease, the polar opposite of the dis-ease state that stress imposes.

The effects of laughter can last for several minutes afterwards because it triggers the release or endorphins and serotonin, the "feel good" chemicals.

Have you ever caught yourself laughing out loud at a book you're reading or a video you're watching in a crowded waiting room filled with people on their cell phones?

Did you find that in no time people were looking up smiling or laughing with you?

Why is that?

Is laughter such a welcomed distraction or is it a hidden desire to connect to one another?

Aha! – Emotional distractions deserve attention.

"Humour and laughter are infectious and can bring people together and make them forget their troubles and one of the best tools to maintain a positive outlook and good health," writes Mack Lemouse in *Health Guidance*. "Laughter is also correlated with mental health and has many social and interpersonal benefits. With all these benefits, laughter is an antidepressant, pain killer, workout, stress reliever and a great way to make friends and strengthen bonds."

I know "work" is a four-letter word but the good news is that we get to work with others. People can give us our greatest sense of connectivity and belonging.

If laughter is our common denominator with endless benefits, then bring it on!!

I'll start.

I just read a book about helium. It was so good I can't put it down!

Action: What's your favourite joke or funny story? Write it down, practice it, then share it with everyone you see today.

_____

_____

_____

_____

_____

_____

_____

_____

_____

_____

_____

_____

_____

_____

_____

_____

_____

_____

_____

Did you ever see the movie, "What Women Want"?

It's a funny movie about a male advertising executive who gets electrocuted, having tripped and fallen into the bathtub while trying out a number of women's products. Ooops, sorry – that's not the funny part!

When he wakes up – wearing pantyhose, nail enamel, eye makeup, and having waxed his legs – he realizes he can actually hear what women are thinking. At first it's his housekeeper he hears (she found him in grand style in the morning). What she says to him and what she says to herself are surely different! But he hears them both.

On his way to work that day he continues to pick up thoughts from the concierge at his condo, women on the running trail and from each and every female colleague in the office. He even forges a great relationship with his teenage daughter with his new-found ability to tap into her mind as well.

Initially it drives him crazy, constantly hearing women's inner dialogue and not being able to escape it. Eventually he uses what he hears to successfully collaborate with the female Creative Director in the firm. They won their biggest account – Nike – with a brilliant campaign for women's sports apparel.

Most of us don't have the ability to know what others are thinking. But when it's important to serve a market, gain a buyer, build a team, support your mate or motivate your kid, asking questions is your magic key.

Aha! – When we speak, we already know what we're going to say. When we listen, we learn.

Assuming everyone thinks the way we do is doomsday in the making.

As enthusiastic as we may be about a product, a methodology, a tool, a destination, a tech device, a sport, a wine, a book or any number of things, that doesn't mean it suits the person you wish to engage. By asking specific questions, then listening openly and without judgment, you have the info to design your offer in a way to meet your target bang-on.

Sounds easy but, I promise, it's not. What's easy is to impose your conditioning and preferences. THAT feels natural. After all, if we like it, they'll like it… right? WRONG!

When you want to succeed in gaining another's attention, the focus needs to be on them. Ask a question, "be vewy, vewy quiet" and witness the kingdom doors opening up.

Would you like a personalized key chain to go with that magic key?

Action: Who do you know that has the key to the information you're seeking? What would you ask them? See them out then listen — really listen — to their answers

_____

_____

_____

_____

_____

_____

_____

_____

_____

_____

_____

_____

_____

_____

_____

_____

_____

_____

I'm a big believer in conducting personality profiles.

In fact, I would go so far as to say they are crucial in creating quality teams.

When you understand each member's style of communication, evaluating, buying, working and socializing, it's far easier to build respectful and cohesive teams.

A cohesive team is a productive team.

A productive team is a happy, profitable team.

Studies show that people are hired on their ability to perform in their role.

Makes sense, right?

But guess what? The main reason people are often released from their roles is because of their personality.

Same is true for employees' decisions. The number one reason people leave jobs is because of issues with their direct supervisor.

Does this mean that when we get along with others we'll be more inspired to do great work?

Aha! – "If he works for you, you work for him." ~ Japanese proverb

What would happen if we all took responsibility for a happy, productive workplace?

Elbert Hubbard said, "It's a fine thing to have ability, but the ability to discover ability in others is the true test."

Let's face it. We can't do anything alone. We all need one another to succeed.

And there isn't any process, machine, computer, or system that doesn't require people to design and operate it.

We do need to be heavily invested in ourselves to deliver our best; but, being cognizant of our ability to fit in means we're also invested in others.

The most basic human desire is to know that you belong… and you do.

Action: Name someone who you may not know well, but that with whom, a better relationship would benefit you both. Outline what you can do to enhance that relationship.

_____

_____

_____

_____

_____

_____

_____

_____

_____

_____

_____

_____

_____

_____

_____

_____

_____

_____

_____

_____

_____

_____

_____

Do you learn deliberately?

I mean, in your day, you always have so much to do. There are constant demands on your time, right?

How challenging is it to actually carve out pockets to feed your mind? It's tough enough to stay "on" the curve never mind ahead of it!

Maybe the question is, "What is the backlash when we don't?"

Just when you think you've mastered your phone, a new model is announced.

Just when you think you've finished your budget, expenditures for upgrades and renovations come into play.

Just when you think your HR program supports your entire team, the government introduces new legislations.

Just when you think your marketing plan is iron-clad, new surveys show a shift in buying patterns.

Aha! – "In times of change learners inherit the earth; while the learned find themselves beautifully equipped to deal with a world that no longer exists." ~ Eric Hoffer

When it comes to your craft "mastery" is an evolving process.

Being an "expert" means you not only have a skilled ability, you are plugged in to change.

It's easy to get so busy "doing" that the idea of "advancing" might seem like we're inviting overload; but "advancing" is the Universe's intention for us.

Growth is inherent in our nature.

In fact it's startling when we realize we can do w-a-y more than for what we give ourselves credit.

Here's an idea: When you write in your gratitude journal, add what you're thankful for learning today.

And stay curious.

Action: Identify one important source of learning. In gratitude, describe how that knowledge or experience supports your growth.

I couldn't help but capture a conversation between two students a while back.

One was on her way to work and said she didn't have time to chat, but time lagged on. She continued her conversation with her friend knowing full well she'd be late for work.

While she shared that she was satisfied to have the job ("It paid the bills"), she nonetheless complained about her job. She is in sales at a cell phone store. One of her issues one day was that her boss questioned her being on Facebook with her friends while she was supposed to be working. She explained that she had met her quota and didn't know what his problem was.

$Aha!$ – "There are no traffic jams on the extra mile." ~ Zig Ziglar

The extra mile is surely the road less travelled and I believe it's because most people don't see the value in it.

Here it is:

First you work for yourself, then you work for someone else.

You see you don't really get paid "by" someone, you get paid "through" someone. Your compensation is directly connected to the value you bring to the table.

Limit your value. Limit your compensation.

But it's even bigger than that.

When YOU hold value in what you do, you take care to do your very best job regardless of the pay or circumstances. This is about building character. If you remember 10th grade science class, energy is never destroyed. Energy is also never wasted. When you invest your energy in yourself, in developing your skills and willingness to do your best, you will always be held in high regard: first by you, then by others. Oh and here's the important part. It's your regard that matters most.

My student friend in the cell phone job is a bright girl studying law.

I just know that when she gets herself, she'll set the world on fire!

Action: What is one area in which you may be holding back because it may not appear worthwhile? What value can you add in that area?

_____
_____
_____
_____
_____
_____
_____
_____
_____
_____
_____
_____
_____
_____
_____
_____
_____
_____
_____
_____
_____

A friend of mine, who developed a national anti-bullying campaign in his home country, was telling me how disappointed he was that his own daughter was being bullied in school. Apparently she attended a private school, one that was receiving the awareness material and engaged in the anti-bullying campaign. Didn't matter. Her hearing impairment made her a fun target for her peers who somehow felt superior.

We talk about bullying as though it only exists in the school yard.

I suppose educating kids on why it's wrong is a good place to start, yet bullying is so prevalent in the adult world, too.

Sometimes it's disguised.

I had a conversation with the owner of one of our manufacturing facilities. He shared how often they develop product ideas for customers just for those very ideas to be shared with other factories (in search of a cheaper price) or for the effort invested to be disregarded, developed internally or not paid for. (Has this ever happened to you?)

I think on some level that's bullying.

The definition of bullying is "To use superior strength or influence to intimidate (someone), typically to force him or her to do what one wants."

Aha! – With power comes responsibility.

The responsibility lies in how you're going to use that power with respect to the people with whom you engage for your success.

The law of cause and effect says what goes around comes around. And it doesn't always come from the same source or in the same way, but it does return, like a boomerang.

By taking care to value and acknowledge the efforts of others who invest in you, you're actually setting a precedent as to how YOU want to be treated.

I know. It's deep.

But think of it this way. Life is like a mirror. Everything you send out reflects back.

By acknowledging and respecting the people who support your success, you're actually sending out powerful good wishes for yourself!

So cool how the Universe works.

Action: Elaborate on a time when you felt bullied or undervalued, then pledge to not pay that forward — ever.

Do you like gifts?

Crazy question, right?

Isn't it the best feeling when someone gives you something thoughtful for no anticipated reason?

I was on the dance floor of an event years ago.

A friend danced up to me and told me she absolutely loved my jacket.

I handed it to her to try on and she went spinning around like a princess.

She looked great in the jacket so I told her she could keep it.

Once she picked her jaw up off the floor she hugged me, then herself in her new jacket, and all smiles, continued to spin around the dance floor.

I'm not sure if it was she or I who was more excited.

Aha! – Enhancing another's life enhances ours.

We're wired to help one another.

In an article entitled *5 Ways Giving Is Good for You* By Jill Suttie and Jason Marsh, December 13, 2010, the writers cite a 2006 study by Jorge Moll and colleagues at the National Institute of Health: "When people give to charities, it activates regions of the brain associated with pleasure, social connection, and trust, creating a 'warm glow' effect. Scientists also believe that altruistic behavior releases endorphins in the brain, producing the positive feeling known as the 'helper's high.'"

A 2008 study by Harvard Business School professor Michael Norton and colleagues found that giving money to someone else lifted participants' happiness more than spending it on themselves (despite participants' prediction that spending on themselves would make them happier).

"How about them apples?" (as my dad would say) We feel better gifting someone else than we do ourselves.

While it's important to feed ourselves – life is for living – sharing is in our DNA.

Christmas is coming. Surprise a few extra people this year… for you.

Action: Think of an individual or an organization that you respect and why. What small gesture can you take that would be a welcomed surprise to them and make you feel on top of the world?

Everything has an opposite.

There is no up without a down. There's no black without a white. There's no in without an out. It's nature.

We, too, have opposites in our personality. It's what keeps us balanced.

We exude strengths in different areas but have the opposing strength in existence and can draw on it at any time.

In fact, my business coach, Paul Fini, always says, "An overused strength becomes a weakness."

(I'll give you a second to think about that one ... it's so true!)

Sometimes those opposites in our personality can be our greatest attributes or create our biggest hurdles.

When my son was golfing competitively, sometimes the not-so-supportive side of his personality would arise after a bad shot and sabotage his next one. The cheerleading, "you can do it" voice was too quiet and the "you suck" voice was stronger. I used to suggest to my son that he humanize the voices; pretend that they each were little people sitting on his shoulders. Recognize them – don't fight them. And when the negative person would chirp, reach over and simply flick him off his shoulder. Let him know you have a game to play and that his comments aren't welcome. Listen, instead, to the cheerleader.

Aha! – The opposing voices both belong to us which means we can choose to which we listen.

I recently had a bracelet engraved with "infinite potential" to remind me what I'm capable of. It's a physical symbol with a powerful message that will help to keep the voice that challenges my desires, in check.

Opposites exist in us. It's part of who we are.

What's important to recognize is that our results are a reflection of our self-talk. Choose the good stuff.

Action: When your negative self-talker chimes in, what is he or she saying to you? Describe something you can do or say to override that voice and stay positive.

Isn't it frustrating when you really, really want something to happen then it doesn't?

Like you set a goal, work towards it, expect it, and it doesn't seem to materialize?

What's the hold up?

All the conditions seem to be ideal, yet the goal just isn't manifesting.

The issue could be you!

Let me explain.

Sometimes your own belief in yourself is a stumbling block to your accomplishments.

While you might have created a clear mental picture of what that goal looks like, the goal somehow doesn't feel natural. Maybe it's a stretch beyond what you think you deserve.

Aha! – We don't achieve our goals, we grow into them.

The truth is you have to be mentally ready to accept the goal by becoming the person the goal requires you to be!!

This is huge!

Les Brown – The Millionaire Motivator – was said, "You don't get in life what you want; you get in life what you are, and that's why we must invest in ourselves..."

It's not about being separate from your goal but embodying your goal emotionally and preparing yourself as a person to own the goal.

Make sense?

Of all the investments you can make, the one where you invest in YOU can yield the greatest impact.

Your goal will manifest only when YOU are ready.

Oh, and by the way, you're totally worth it.

Action: First, have a look down the side of that mountain you're climbing to see just how far you've come. Looking upward, what characteristics do you need to develop to make it to the peak?

_____

_____

_____

_____

_____

_____

_____

_____

_____

_____

_____

_____

_____

_____

_____

_____

_____

_____

_____

While my son was in middle school I attended a presentation at the high school.

The presenter was a teacher of teachers and shared with the parents the teaching style of the future.

He said that in this age of information availability, "facilitators" will go the way of the dinosaurs.

The reason being that with the click of a mouse we can access whatever information we need!

We don't need someone to simply read from a text book or power point slides.

But I'm not sure all teachers got the memo.

In fact my friend Stacey has been on a work-related course all week and the unfortunate victim of boring facilitators.

Remember that teacher growing up that actually inspired you to learn and experience?

You walked away from their class feeling like something changed in you?

$Aha!$ – Teaching is not the filling of the pail but the lighting of the fire.

It's certainly my sentiment but William Butler Yeats' words.

Why do I mention this?

I believe teachers can be change agents.

I also believe we are all teachers.

We teach with our knowledge. We inspire with our passion.

The next time you're asked to present, do so willingly.

And consider less the content and more the enthusiasm for what you're sharing.

YOU bring the brilliance to the room.

Action: Think of a time when you hesitated to accept an opportunity to deliver a message because you were concerned what people might think. Rewrite the hesitation with acceptance and then journal what the positive outcome would look like.

When speaking at Bob Proctor's Matrixx, Gina gave everyone a card to start the day that said, "It's the START that STOPS most people."

It's a quote by Don Shula and isn't it true?

Taking that very first step towards something new can feel so heavy.

There is surely no shortage of good ideas, aspirations and goals floating around.

But what happens when we try and take that first step?

Often a mountain of fear appears and stops us in our tracks.

Fear can be such a deterrent in us achieving our potential.

That quote prompted me to re-read Susan Jeffers' book, *Feel the Fear and Do It Anyway* in conjunction with some work I'm doing on making a difference.

She says, "The only way to feel better about myself is to go out… and do it."

Aha! – **"Do the thing and you'll get the energy to do the thing."** ~ Ralph Waldo Emerson

It sounds like a chicken 'n' egg theory but it's the real deal.

And we get to choose how we work it.

Will it be the "start" or the "stop" that tells our story?

Will we allow fear to paralyze us, or will we conquer fear by stepping out of our own way and into our new, powerful selves?

Goals should be scary and exciting all at the same time.

So here's another thought: could it be that what we're labelling as fear is actually our internal fire, filled with possibility?

Hmmmm, that sounds like a second "aha"!

Today, let's hit the new ground running.

Action: What have you really wanted to do and what excuses do you tell yourself that continue to stop the start? Is today the day you take that first monumental step?

_____

_____

_____

_____

_____

_____

_____

_____

_____

_____

_____

_____

_____

_____

_____

_____

_____

_____

_____

_____

Of my favourite things to own, I love books. One day I will bring all of my books into my office and create a beautiful library.

True that the on-line versions are more portable and convenient, but there is a certain energy in the physical property of a book that, to me, makes it irreplaceable.

I especially love to own books that are signed by their author.

I enjoy listening to the author share their passion. Then, when I read their thoughts on the pages, it's like they're reading to me.

And having the books signed adds to the connection I feel with the author.

I believe everyone has a book in them.

Each and every person's life and experience is so unique and fascinating.

If you were to write a story, what would it be about?

Would it be a mystery? Or a children's book? An insightful guide? Or a how-to?

Who might be inspired by your story?

I've met many an author and equally as many people who have given thought to capturing their gifts on paper – if only casually – but never do.

Sometimes the concept of the project is overwhelming, but many times it's because people don't grasp the value of their voice.

Aha! – Never underestimate the profound effect sharing your story might have.

Good stories are like great songs. You can experience them many times over with an abundance of enjoyment.

And they tend to take a life of their own, potentially affecting people w-a-y beyond your known circle.

While life can throw curve balls sometimes, know that it's all part of your story; one that you'll enjoy sharing one day… right?

Action: Describe a time in your life when what seemed to be the worst thing that happened turned out to be the best. What was that pivotal point?

In an event I co-chaired, the success, in part, resulted in a donation to the local Humane Society.

While the event itself wasn't a fundraiser, we did incorporate some activities into the event to benefit our community partner.

At dinner, when we presented the cheque and BIG heap of cage towels to the HS officials, they jumped up and down and hugged us like we had just given them the keys to the kingdom.

It was adorable to watch.

What happened was that it made us feel like we all had done something super special and everyone was witness that their efforts were gratefully appreciated.

Here's the thing.

While the donation was generous considering the size of the group and will help in the Humane Society's meaningful work, it certainly isn't going to cover their operating budget for any length of time.

It didn't matter.

It was met with enthusiasm and sheer delight.

Aha! – Appreciate everything like it's the first time.

After the event I sent a letter, with pictures attached, to the department heads at the venue appreciating all departments and some specific individuals. It was important to me that they knew my co-chair and I recognized their diligence in bringing our vision to life and that, together, we created an exceptional experience for the attendees.

I've been involved with countless events and witnessed success about as many times.

It doesn't matter.

I wrote the letter like it was a first.

When your employees walk through the door this morning, welcome them back with enthusiasm.

When you take that conference call, marvel in the technology that allows you to communicate instantly around the globe.

Have lunch outside and breathe in the peacefulness and natural abundance that surrounds you.

Mostly, be in awe of yourself… often.

Action: What is one thing you can do today, something that you do every day — like having lunch — where you can be more observant of your circumstances? What will you do? How will you enjoy it like it's the very first time?

_____
_____
_____
_____
_____
_____
_____
_____
_____
_____
_____
_____
_____
_____
_____
_____
_____
_____
_____

When people ask you what business you're in, how do you respond?

Are you in the business of IT?

Are you a food purveyor?

Are you a provider of bedding and towels?

Charles Revson, the founder of Revlon, said about his company, "In the factory, Revlon manufactures cosmetics, but in the store Revlon sells hope."

When the Sales Manager or V.P. of Finance at Revlon reviews the sales reports they would be looking at the numbers of lipsticks, mascaras, and nail enamels they push through.

But Charles Revson understood that while his company brought a commodity to market, it was the emotion behind why people bought that drove the sales.

In, *The E-myth*, Michael E. Gerber asks the question, "What feeling will your customer walk away with? Peace of mind? Order? Power? Love? What is he really buying when he buys from you?"

Aha! – Emotion trumps reason.

Coke® started with, "Drink Coca-cola" as their first advertising slogan in 1886 and moved through a number of tag lines around their drink, like, "Delicious and refreshing", and "Things go better with Coke."

Their slogans in 1917 and 1925 reflected their market dominance: "Three million a day," then "Six million a day."

They tapped into the physical "thirst-quenching" need with, "Refresh yourself" (1924) and, "Be really refreshed" (1959).

Then in 2009 they launched, "Open Happiness."

While Coke® provides bottled beverages, they sell "happiness"… and who doesn't want to be happy??

The term, "solutions" has been incorporated into many corporate missions but it's still somewhat incomplete.

We need to dig deeper and know that the real mission is for your solution to generate a positive emotion.

Think of it like you're being paid in emojis and you'll have the world on your doorstep.

Action:

Describe the emotion you most want to generate as a result of your work.

It's easy to take small things for granted because, after all, they're small!

If they're small they must not have much significance, right?

Not so fast.

Driving today, we realized how many drivers don't use turn signals, like if they want to change lanes or pull into the plaza in front of you.

Flipping on a turn signal is a small thing that makes a big difference in allowing you to plan your drive.

(Of course there are the people who drive for miles with their turn signal on, but we'll save them for another Aha)

Watching the BMW championships, I marveled at the golfers who drive the ball over 300 yards.

Also worth noting is that a one-inch putt counts for the same number on the score card – one stroke – as the 300 yard drive.

The one-inch putt is a small thing, but sinking it can make a big difference to the outcome.

Getting your message across requires good communication skills, especially in the form of punctuation.

In a text that says, "Let's eat, Sally!", omitting the comma to say, "Let's eat Sally!" delivers a completely different meaning!

The comma is a pretty small thing that makes a big difference in the message you deliver.

Aha! – "Be faithful in small things because it is in them that your strength lies." ~ Mother Teresa

Saying, "thank you," taking the stairs instead of the elevator, reading five extra pages, calling ahead, commenting on a post, responding to an invitation, following up, bringing Timmies, staying to watch your kid's lesson, listening, and of course, using your turn signal, might sound like small things but in the grand scheme can have a profound effect.

After all, "Great things are done by a series of small things brought together." ~ Vincent Van Gogh

And we all know you absolutely own greatness.

Action: What one small thing can you commit to doing for the next month that will yield significant results? (BTW, "Timmies," in Canada, is synonymous with "coffee.")

I was at a conference with a magnificent collection of Canadian women presidents.

It was apparent why these women – and others like them – are driving the economy.

They're passionate, collaborative, insightful, talented and just really nice people.

What's fascinating to listen to is how they juggle priorities.

In fact, one of our speakers – an accomplished journalist, now consultant – shared her changing priorities as her family and career grew.

She started one sentence by saying, "When you order your priorities ...." I immediately drifted off for a second, retreating into my thoughts.

I believe the context of her comment was putting priorities in some kind of order but I heard, "order priorities", like you would order breakfast in a drive-thru.

The statement sounded so empowering, alluding to how we can own our schedule.

All too often our best intentions are side-tracked by external forces and we release control.

How do we know when we have effectively ordered priorities?

Aha! – "**Action expresses priorities.**" ∼ Mahatma Gandhi

The sure-fire way to tell where priorities are is in behaviour.

(I think it's section 4, subsection B-1 of the unwritten Human Code of Conduct, under, "Actions speak louder than words")

According to Gandhi, that which we do reflects what is truly our priority.

Whether it's your signature priority like family, integrity, reverse climate change OR a more immediate priority like getting the thank-you cards out the door, dropping 10 pounds, or achieving a sales quota, your aligned actions will signal which priority is owned.

Remember when you "order", you're giving a command with intent and desire.

You wouldn't approach the drive-thru window asking, "May I have something to eat, please?" You'd be more specific and expect what's in the package to match the order.

Ask yourself, "May I take your order?", then put yourself in drive!

Action: List your top 10 values then prioritize them. What action do you routinely take on priority #1?

Remember being on the teeter totter when you were seven?

Likely you didn't have the strength to pick up your friend all by yourself but on a teeter totter, you had no problem lifting her up higher than you! If you were about the same size, the fulcrum – positioned right in the middle of the plank – allowed you both to easily move each other up and down. Then your 12-year-old brother showed up and replaced your friend at her end of the teeter totter, and being the prankster that he was, kept you in the air for what seemed like eternity!

There was no way your feet were going to touch the ground until he decided so. Unfortunately for you, the fulcrum was strategically placed in the centre of the see-saw and put you at a disadvantage.

Now had the fulcrum been positioned further towards your brother's end, the additional length of the plank on your side would have allowed you to prop him up! That's the law of levers. You can potentially exert a small force at one end of the lever to move a large load at the other end.

One small change – a shift in the fulcrum positioning – would have allowed you and your seven-year-old effort, to hoist your big brother.

The first order of levers says that when you position the effort further from the load, you need less effort to move the load. The lever becomes a force magnifier!!

Just think what it would mean to be able to magnify your efforts in more circumstances. Oh wait – you can!!

Let's say, for instance, you've just learned some shocking news that of the 960 kids in the primary school in your neighbourhood, 20% of them go to school without breakfast.

"That just shouldn't be so!" says you, but reality is, feeding 192 kids at approximately $4.00 each per day X the number of school days seems like an insurmountable sum and potentially an enormous amount of effort! So… do you walk away from the school ground or do you leverage yourself to tackle an issue important to you?

Aha! – Rather than seeing yourself as the effort, see yourself as the fulcrum.

Quite possibly you're not in a position to make 192 kids breakfast every day, so assuming the role of "effort" might cause you to give up. But since the issue is too important to you, reposition yourself as the fulcrum, giving leverage to others to jump on board.

Where the fulcrum is placed determines how much effort would be required to move the load.

Once you determine the magnitude of the load, you're in an ideal position to calculate the effort required, and the more people or resources you bring on board, the less effort is required by everyone.

Leveraging yourself is like strapping on that super hero cape… and we both know the world needs more heroes.

Action: What is one effect you want to have on humankind? What existing group could you inspire or partner with to achieve that effect?

Do you remember the story about the tortoise and the hare?

Here's the Cole's notes as a refresher.

The hare boasted about being so swift and the tortoise, tired of hearing it, challenged the hare to a race saying, "...even you can be beat".

Now I know you already know the ending – the tortoise won – but it's what happened in the middle that is worthy of our attention.

You see, the hare, figuring he had the race in the bag, took time for a nap, then lunch, then another nap, and eventually awoke to see the tortoise a yard from the finish line. Even though the hare bolted to catch up – tongue hanging out, exhausted from the stretch – the tortoise crossed the finish line first.

Now the tortoise told the hare at the finish line, "Slowly does it every time".

But did speed have anything to do with who won the race?

Or was it consistent effort that won?

There may be days that you don't feel like cooking healthy food to stay on your diet (easier to swing through the drive-thru) or mornings where the weather isn't conducive to enjoying your run. There are days when meetings consume time that you really need to practice your presentation or reacting to family requests steal thinking time for that article you've been meaning to publish.

Aha! – **"Never let the urgent crowd out the important."**
~ Kelly Caitlin Walker

We all have the same 24 hours in a day. It's how we choose to invest our time that will pay dividends relative to our goals.

Having a clearly stated goal is a first step.

But, in order to achieve it, you must even more clearly outline what you're willing to commit to – CONSISTENTLY.

Rome wasn't built in a day.

Building yourself requires your attention – and you keeping your promises to yourself – every single day.

#beyourbestyou

Action:

What one thing can you do consistently, every day that over the span of a year will have a profound effect on your success?

_____

_____

_____

_____

_____

_____

_____

_____

_____

_____

_____

_____

_____

_____

_____

_____

_____

_____

_____

If you were to follow in the footsteps of the best in your industry, who would that be?

Would it be the largest organization in terms of employees?

Does your definition include number of offices or multi-country presence?

Is it the one with the greatest sales volume or the trendiest products?

Is it the most profitable player?

If you wanted to be the "best" in your industry, what would "best" look like?

In an interview I listened to this morning featuring a CEO of a North American organization, he defined the" best" in his industry by the ones who aren't afraid.

He elaborated that when someone isn't afraid – they're willing to invest in themselves, innovate, collaborate (even with competitors), build from their core competencies, and look for new ways to serve their clients – they're sustainable.

Aha! – Sustained success is value-based.

You see all of what this CEO described in his term of "best" isn't always quantifiable. Their companies are built, and their industry respect derived, from their values.

When you dare to wear your values – even your vulnerability – like a badge of uniqueness, and then stay open to possibilities, your company continually morphs into its very own version of "best".

Competing means that one day you win, then the next day someone else wins.

Creating means you own your own space and ultimately your destiny.

Boldly go where no brand has gone before.

Action:

How do your values play a part?

_____

_____

_____

_____

_____

_____

_____

_____

_____

_____

_____

_____

_____

_____

_____

_____

_____

_____

_____

_____

_____

_____

_____

Did you ever notice that the people who have neat files in their offices also have trunk organizers in their cars and glasses in their kitchen cupboards lined up like little soldiers?

And do you know executives who hold their colleagues, customers and competitors equally in high regard?

What about those who are on time – or late. The early birds show up within a time that allows them to easily meet their commitment and the tardy souls fly in frantically at the last minute… every single time.

I played golf with someone for the first time the other day. I couldn't help but notice how very supportive and complimentary he was to each individual in our group, but put an enormous amount of pressure on himself.

Knowing that he is a business owner, it made me wonder if he drives himself hard to support his customers and team.

The common thread? We can't hide who we are.

Aha! – How you do one thing is how you do everything.

We all have a range of strengths on which to draw to handle any circumstance, but it's a combination of our values and choices that drive how we handle those circumstances.

People who are leaders in the workplace are often the first to help out in an emergency or step up to drive a charity initiative.

People who have respect for the planet recycle regardless of where they are and are consistent with their compassion for all living things.

People who value time will mind theirs as they do others and rarely take either for granted.

You are always offering subtle hints as to who you are; sometimes in your words, and always in your actions.

It's when the two align that you are in integrity and your true awesomeness shines through.

Being true to yourself never felt so good, eh?

Action:

What action do you do that causes you to feel resentment? How can you shift that perspective so the effort feels good?

How much can you trust advertising messages?

If the advertiser says their product will work three times faster, or save you $2500 per year or make you look 10 years younger, how much of that message compels you to buy it?

In years past, an advertiser's message was the primary way in which we learned about a product.

And campaigns were easy to measure. The owner of the product ran a commercial, an ad or conducted a mail order campaign.

We bought the message and bought the product (or not) and it was super easy to track.

In today's world, a marketer's job is so much more complex.

It's not only because there are a multitude of ways in which to share your message- on-line media alone offers a plethora of channels – but it's the opportunity that consumers and customers have to verify the advertisers' message that makes the difference.

Consider this. You send out a message about a new product or service. What might your customer do next?

Google it?

Google your company?

Search for reviews?

Read an article or blog about your product or company?

Compare the product on different channels?

Put their intent to purchase on Facebook to see what their friends have to say?

What are they looking for?

Aha! – **"I find that when you open the door toward openness and transparency, a lot of people will follow you through."**
~ Kirsten Gillibrand

It's still true that people buy from people they like and trust.

And what better way to build trust than to be transparent about what you sell, how you serve, and what to expect?

While your advertising message may have been the buying stimulant, there are countless influencing factors that bring the sale to your doorstep.

Transparency is your brand's BFF.

Action: What can you share in a post or blog that would offer an insightful glimpse of what goes on behind the scenes in your life or your organization?

Remember when we were little and we would "pretend"?

In our fantasy at play we could be anything or anyone we wanted to.

We were moms to our dolls, teachers to our friends, ninjas to our siblings, and princesses… just because.

Our imagination was vivid and we welcomed it to take us wherever it did.

What happened?

Okay, so we grew up, but is that a reason to stop the fantasy?

I remember when my son was about 7, he and his friends used to love to play spy games. They had all kinds of spy gear and would hide behind couches and planters. They'd communicate through walkie talkies about what was going on in the house and document it all on "spy pads" (way before kids' cell phones). To them they were invisible and on a mission. Their imagination turned our home into the perfect scene for curiosity. My cookie baking could cause quite a stir!

"Fantasy" is not considered adult behaviour. We might allow ourselves to "brainstorm" but we put a lid on letting our minds travel.

And if for a moment someone does allow their thoughts to take them into another dimension, they don't dare share them.

There will be far more people who criticize, squash, obstruct, ridicule even sabotage ideas than support them.

So we suppress our creativity and label ourselves "responsible" and "realistic".

Aha! – Sometimes we're too "adult" for our own good.

Walt Disney called it "imagineering". While we celebrate him as a household name in animation and story-telling, it wasn't that way in the beginning. In his early days of cartooning, he struggled to pay his rent and be appropriately compensated for his brilliantly creative work. When Walt tried to get MGM studios to distribute *Mickey Mouse* in 1927 he was told that the idea would never work. There are equally challenging stories about *The Three Little Pigs, Bambi, Fantasia* and a host of Disney's other creations.

Fortunately for us he never stopped imagineering and pressed forward when he knew he had something valuable to share.

The most important part about fantasizing or dreaming or imagineering, is that you don't have to know how you're going to achieve your dream.

In fact, if you did, it wouldn't be a dream, it would just be a plan.

You create the "what" and let the universe take care of the "how".

As Bob Proctor always says, "If you can see it in your mind you can hold it in your hand."

Where will your mind take you today?

Action: What are you holding back doing because you can't figure out how to do it?

Have you ever dealt with someone whose responsibility it was to get back to you with information, then didn't? Maybe it's just me but there are times when I'm waiting to receive prices or project details or contact information, and, well, it just doesn't arrive.

When people fail to respond with something they promised I often ask if what I requested was within their field of responsibility. I think it's a very fair question because sometimes a person – bless their heart – in their effort to be accommodating, will stick their neck out to help but it's not really in their job description to do so. So that task is more difficult or frustrating, never makes their to-do list, and I'm left waiting on someone who is not responsible to me.

But I'm wondering if the question lies more around being accountable as opposed to being responsible. Do you need to be responsible to be accountable?

Aha! – **Responsibility is pre-task, accountability is post-task.**

A job description can outline a field of responsibility – like doing estimates – but accountability is ensuring the estimate is delivered… by whoever is responsible. Make sense?

When people whose responsibility it's not fail to respond, they can take two stances:

1) Blame their position, co-workers, knowledge, work load, the system or any number of things to fall into the role of "victim" and excuse their actions; or

2) Answer for their actions – or lack of same – and be accountable to the outcome.

The bummer about being a "victim" is that you give your power away – someone else controls your outcome – and it turns out you don't need a title to be a leader!

Everyone has "mis-takes" but it's how you respond – "Take two!" – to what didn't go quite right the first time, that shows leadership. According to John C. Maxwell, "A leader is one who knows the way, goes the way, and shows the way."

Even if what you promised doesn't lie in your field of responsibility, you likely "know the way" to someone who can help make good on your promise. "Management is doing things right; leadership is doing the right things." ~ Peter Drucker

"Right, right, you're bloody-well right…"

Action: What one thing did you promise and not deliver? Can you be accountable by assigning the responsibility to someone else?

What was the first thing that popped into your head this morning?

You might have been a bit groggy or, if you're like me, startled by the alarm, but what is the first thing you remembered saying to yourself?

Something like:

"Ugh – I'm so tired!"

"I'm never going to make that meeting in time!"

"I really don't feel like going to the gym in the dark!"

"This is going to be a demanding day!"

If you told yourself anything like the above – and I'll ask the classic psychologists' question here – how did that make you feel?

Were you energized to get up and get going with your day??

Now maybe you woke up with the sun shining and birds chirping and with a sense of gratitude in your heart looking forward to a magnificent day! If that was you, how did *that* make you feel?

When I share what I'm working on with my friend and coach, Peggy McColl, she always says, "I see you accomplishing that easily."

Now she obviously believes in me, which, in itself, is a huge gift, and when she uses the word "easily", I immediately relax and have a calm sense of knowing; I move confidently forward.

If Peggy asked me, "What hurdles do you have to overcome?", or "What part of your goal stresses you out?" then I would surely assume a different posture and frame of mind.

Aha! – That which you tell yourself affects your belief.

It's not like there won't be parts of your day or your goal process that aren't going to stretch or challenge but it's the **words** you choose to describe them that sets your attitude in motion. You can frame the challenges as potential "struggles" which would make you feel like you're in for a painful process OR You can frame the challenges as potential "growth" which would make you feel like you're expanding your mind and spirit.

If you tell yourself that you'll never find a parking spot, then you won't.

If you tell yourself that you'll get a cold every Christmas, then you will.

If you tell yourself that you're wasting your time, have no control, aren't lucky, will not have a good time at the party, aren't ready for your presentation or any other negative thing, you will own those issues as well.

Your subconscious mind is programmed to believe whatever you tell yourself. Given who you are and that you have the gifts of higher faculties –will, reason, imagination, intuition, and memory – you're a power-house package that can handle anything!

So what's your big opportunity today?

I see you accomplishing that "easily".

Action: Start a sentence about a challenging circumstance with, "I never..." and end it with "...until now." e.g. "I never get the help I need... until now." Claim what you need.

What's your legacy?

What is it that people say about you when you're not in the room?

Now I'm not talking about the day-to-day comments like, "I'm really happy for her new promotion," or "He made a great point in our meeting today."

I mean the bigger comments about your vibrant character and how you affect people.

Now if you look up the word legacy, you'll probably get a definition that revolves around money or personal property left in a will.

Some people work their entire lives in order to leave financial security to their family, their church, a charity, their local hospital or special friends.

Do we evaluate a person's contribution to humankind – their legacy – by the amount of earnings they leave behind?

What about their artistic legacy, legacy project or legacy of love and respect?

Aha! – Your legacy is all of what makes you memorable.

When you leave the room people probably say how you always make them smile, that you have a good head on your shoulders, that you're a giving and generous person or that you make a great dad.

The more you expand your unique talents and abilities, to bring joy to yourself and positively affect humankind, the more you're living your legacy.

And the more meaning you give your life, the more life you'll give to that meaning... for a long time to come.

Live large.

Action: Pretend you walked into a conversation where a group of people were talking about your life's work. What are they saying about you?

_____
_____
_____
_____
_____
_____
_____
_____
_____
_____
_____
_____
_____
_____
_____
_____
_____
_____
_____

Did you know that gossip can make you gain weight?

Here's the logic.

Gossip is typically negative and is often born of something that is making us uneasy or stressed. When we're uneasy or stressed, we release cortisol – the "stress hormone" – into our blood stream. Stress, especially long-term, chronic stress, actually boosts your hunger and when you're stressed you release more cortisol. That causes higher insulin levels. Your blood sugar drops and you crave sugary, fatty foods.

"More stress = more cortisol = higher appetite for junk food = more belly fat," says Shawn M. Talbott, PhD, a nutritional biochemist.

The correlation between gossip and weight gain goes even deeper than that.

You know that we're "energy beings", right??

Well, negative words carry a lower vibration compared to positive words that have a high vibration.

"Our energy can move at a very high vibrational frequency which will bring us more health, happiness and prosperity, or at a very low vibrational frequency, which will bring us the opposite." ~ Andrea Schulman, creator of "Raise Your Vibration Today".

So can the water cooler conversations be bringing you down??

Aha! – Be good to yourself by saying good about others.

According to Schulman, other symptoms that your vibration might be low include insomnia, frequent accidents, poverty, multiple injuries, dysfunctional relationships and even dandruff!

And it all stems from your vibrational state.

Now, there are a number of things that can affect your vibration but your thoughts, and the words you use to express them, are definite contributors. Schulman says that symptoms of low vibration, "...are simply signs that are meant to show you that you are in a disconnected state, nothing more."

Apparently releasing negativity and going with the flow a bit more, puts you in harmony with the health, prosperity and great relationships you're seeking!

Look for the good stuff. You're worth it.

Action: Make a list of attributes of someone close to you. What one nice thing about them can you share today?

I pulled a bottle of Kefir from the fridge to add to my smoothie and it had expired.

I added some protein powder but it wasn't the same. Kefir is back on the shopping list.

Then I read an article that said mayonnaise shouldn't be kept more than a few months once it's opened and that nuts, because of their oils, lose their freshness in about the same amount of time.

And so much for keeping a first aid kit current. Fortunately we rarely open it but the last time we did, the ointment in there had expired as well.

I went to pick up some new golf balls with a coupon I was saving. When I got to the check-out counter, I realized it, too, had expired.

When you're busy, days and weeks seem to slip by so quickly that expiry dates just come and go!

The good news is that the dates are stamped in a prominent place. Be it milk or medication, the "best before..." date is clearly visible. The older the product, the less likely it is to be optimum.

Is it a good thing or a bad thing that we don't know our personal expiry date?

We all have one – there are only so many grains of sand in the hour glass – but does that "best before..." date being a mystery cause us to mentally wrongly position our optimum level?

Do we allow our age, another individual or society to influence when our "best" actually is?

Aha! – **"It doesn't matter where you are, you are nowhere compared to where you can go."** ~ Bob Proctor

Every experience you endure, every person with whom you converse, every chance you take on yourself, creates your NEW best self.

The Dalai Lama reminds us, "The goal is not to be better than the other man, but your previous self."

It's all about Perspective.

Action: In which area do you tend to compare yourself to others? Now write a sentence that includes your unique combination of attributes that makes you beyond compare.

_____

_____

_____

_____

_____

_____

_____

_____

_____

_____

_____

_____

_____

_____

_____

_____

_____

_____

_____

_____

_____

_____

_____

_____

Would you rather be right or would you rather be rich?

Whether it's a simple report, a special event, re-tooling to take on a new market or running the entire organization, one common success element is to start with a clear vision.

For your report to have clarity, your event to accomplish results, your new market initiative to get traction or your entire organization to scale, clarity of what that end result looks like, is crucial. In building your vision you're on the lookout for people to create circumstances that support your vision and build your success.

After all it's your vision and you know what's right, right?

Aha! – **There can be a fine line between having a clear vision and being attached to an outcome; the line being the difference between being right or being rich.**

Here's the thing: when you're stuck on your vision to the point of being inflexible, those blinders could potentially shut out the very people whose input can help build your dream.

In a conversation my son and I had the other day about everything happening for a reason, William quoted Steve Jobs in saying, "You can only connect the dots backwards." In other words you don't always know what elements – people, circumstances, set-backs, opportunities, time – will determine your course of action and bring you to the realization of your worthy goals, but when you look back you'll see how each of those elements contributed to your success. Had you not been open to those elements, achieving your desired result may well have been hindered.

Marcel Schwantes, principal and founder of Leadership From the Core, identifies that successful leaders, like Steve Jobs, seek wisdom from others and encourage feedback from their team. You're not expecting that all the feedback or advice will be relevant or directly useful but the conversations themselves may spark new ideas or connections you couldn't have reached on your own.

Have a look at the tree in your backyard. Its roots were born of nature's vision but it's the tree's flexibility within the elements that allows it to reach its rich potential.

And being rich is way more fun.

Action:

Name five people who may comprise a great advisory council for you. What would be the first question you would ask them?

_____
_____
_____
_____
_____
_____
_____
_____
_____
_____
_____
_____
_____
_____
_____
_____
_____
_____
_____

Is it unfair to judge a book by its cover?

Do you remember the last time you went to Chapters to pick up a resource for a new initiative or swung by the kiosk at the airport to secure a great read for the airplane ride? Likely you read the back cover to check out the author's credibility and endorsements to ensure the book was a fit for you, but what made you pick up that book in the first place? Was it the title? The colour pattern? The photo or graphic? Probably some combination of the aforementioned was what sparked your curiosity.

Colours have energy. Fonts have meaning. Pictures inspire emotion. Symbols tell a story in themselves. Publishers go to great lengths ensuring that the combination of these available tools are effectively used to capture the attention of their audience and help get their book picked up first.

Figuratively, how often do we judge people by their "covers"? It's not untypical that the well-groomed person with presence can rally the attention of a crowd better than someone with a less charismatic appearance, but is it them or is it us?

Aha! – **"100% of the time your audience defines appropriateness and not you."** ~ Sola Adelowo, AICI CIC, Professional presence thought leader in Treviso, Italy

Yes, of course, you want to be true to yourself and be expressive with your wear but in an article to get people talking about workplace fashion and executive presence, Sola says, "When you meet your audience's expectations, you get instant credibility and are more likely to accomplish your goals and so much more."

Judging is a subconscious thing. Patterns, colours and styles have meaning and effect. Did you know that the traditional jacket was designed to direct focus to your face, where your message is being delivered? That's not to say that you need to wear a jacket to be heard; in fact, you need to be sensitive to the environment and know what dress is appropriate. The ability of a leader to adapt is subliminally shared in their adaptive style of dress.

The BIG point (and you "control freaks" will love this) is that when you understand the signals you give off by how you package your presence, you realize you have the power to direct onlookers' attention to where you need them to pay attention: on your message.

Just like the book, impressions matter, which makes it more than okay to talk "fashion" in the workplace, especially if you're serious about those goals of yours.

Action:

What event is coming up at which you want to make a significant impression? List every article of clothing you plan to wear that day. Missing something? Buy it, find it, borrow it — just get it.

What are you waiting for?

What is consuming your time – keeping you busy – that is distracting you from you work? I don't mean your "job", I mean your "work" – the stuff that flames are made of.

Maybe it's a social media profile that you're dying to reinvent, or the blog sharing your unique insights that's currently all bottled up, the painting class that is yet to receive your registration, the small business plan waiting to be brought into focus from all those notes or the conference that keeps getting postponed.

I'm not for a minute suggesting that you need to jump ship from your current position to ignite the flame; in fact your "work" may very well be more fully revealed by voluntarily stretching the boundaries of your position.

Is there some deep-seeded fear that keeps surfacing in excuses sounding like, "I tried once before and it didn't work.", "I just don't know how to do it." , "They won't listen to me because I'm not in that business.", "It might mean more work for me.", "I don't know the right person.", "I haven't perfected it yet." or everyone's favourite, "I don't have time."?

Is "resistance" building creative, little white lies that fill your time and keep you from delivering more of YOU?

Aha! – Mind your mind more than your excuses.

It's a common saying that our biggest fear is public speaking when, in fact, our biggest fear is looking stupid. We'll often resist looking stupid at all cost. Seth Godin, successful entrepreneur and author of more than a dozen life-changing books says in Linchpin, "The resistance gets its next excuse ready in advance." It's like waves of active excuses ready to support why you can't do something at any given time. You tell yourself the excuses are real but your soul knows otherwise.

Picture a footbridge that crosses the Creek of Fear. On one side of the bridge is "safety" – where routine lives – and on the other side, "freedom". There's not much to the bridge – in fact it swings above a creek that splashes up waves of excuses continuously. Crossing the bridge the first time from the side of safety is a little unnerving, especially if you focus on the waves. And even when you put one foot carefully in front of the other, there is still no guarantee you will land perfectly on the other side. But each attempt is an experience and each experience is a gift in freeing another valuable piece of you.

Seth says that if you want to make a difference you must first make a firm commitment to your idea then set a hard-and-fast date… carved in stone… non-negotiable. It's when you allow passion and conviction to drive you to that deadline, that you make a difference.

…97, 98, 99, 100! Ready or not, here I come!!

Action:

What have you been talking about doing for a while now but haven't? Outline that commitment, set a date, sign it, then pull the trigger. Nothing creates momentum like action.

If you have a chequing account whereby you keep a minimum balance, you are likely earning interest.

Conversely, if you have a mortgage or line of credit or any other borrowed money, you're likely *paying* interest.

Then of course there is interest on credit cards, interest in investments and interest that your sharp kid charges you when you forgot you borrowed $20 from his piggy bank.

One way or another, money has a way of commanding our interest.

It's a given – an accepted practice – that somehow, somewhere money will generate interest.

What about OUR interest?

Is it a given that in other aspects of our lives – physical, mental or spiritual – that we're operating from a point of interest?

If that's the case then why do we eat foods with chemicals, spend more time with our smart phones than our friends, and limit our time in nature?

Are those actions and attitudes in our best interest?

Aha! – **"Thinking about our interest opens up our thinking to include those things that will enhance our lives."**
~ Kathy Petrowsky, Ph.D.

According to Kathy in her recent edition of: *Decisive Moments*, when you operate from a point of wants and needs – vs. from a point of interest – you are focused on what is familiar which tends to be limited and limiting.

The habits and relationships you develop from a perspective of wants and needs don't always serve your interest.

So, what IS your interest?

Is it to develop your talents and abilities as well as your relationships with your family members, colleagues and associates? And does your interest have anything to do with living a healthy, active lifestyle and enjoying all the landscape and culture that our amazing planet has to offer?

If you ever thought that acting in your own best interest was selfish, listen to Kathy's advice. "It is in our interest to care for ourselves, to care for others who are important to us, to develop our talents, and so on. Focusing on our interests confirms that we have a stake in our lives."

Don't you just love the power of choice?

Action:

Committing to having a stake in your own life, describe a habit that needs to be modified in order to live in your best interest.

The big question today is: Did you volunteer?

Did you volunteer to bring in the coffees this morning?

Did you volunteer to work on that big RFP due Friday?

Did you volunteer to review applications, to hit the bank, to write the blog, to order the new computer, to analyze the data, to create the customer profile, to drive a friend to her cancer treatment, to pick up the cheque, to rally event participants, to mentor someone in a new position, to take the kids to practice, to listen to a new idea, to help out with the charity golf tournament… ??

You might be thinking, 'I don't volunteer to go to work, that's what I get paid for! And I don't volunteer to take the kids to practice. If I don't take them, who will? Okay, maybe I volunteer for the charity golf tournament."

Many people feel a sense of obligation to their employer, their team, their family and friends or even their community. And that if there is compensation involved that it's not volunteering.

Have a look at the definition of a volunteer: A person who freely offers to take part in an enterprise or undertake a task.

The definition doesn't say, "A person who takes part for free", it says, "A person who freely offers…"

Volunteering means that you're offering without restriction or interference, that of free will, willingly and readily, openly and honestly. Compensation isn't the deciding factor.

Aha! – Life is the ultimate volunteer sport.

While there may be consequences relative to where, how and to what extent you volunteer, make no mistake, you're always, at the core level, volunteering. "Free will" is one of your maker's greatest gifts.

That means that life is a sum total of your series of choices, your "volunteering", if you will.

So, think about one upcoming effort or undertaking – maybe you need to review applications – and feel for a minute if you're anticipating it or dreading it. Identify the consequences of doing it, not doing it, postponing it, sharing it, or delegating it. Once you decide to do it, realize it's a choice and give it everything you've got, joyfully and enthusiastically.

Volunteer for life.

Action:

How does using the word, "volunteer" (as opposed to "have to" or "need to", or "am expected to") change how you feel about the next task in which you're about to engage?

You've heard the term 'Flight Recorder", right? Its nickname is Black Box (even though they're often painted in "international orange") and they're standard equipment in an aircraft.

Flight Recorders measure everything from pitch, airspeed, altitude, vertical acceleration, hundreds of instruments and internal readings, as well as cockpit conversations.

They make possible the analysis of unusual occurrences by storing performance and condition information.

Now, in our businesses, we, too, employ measurables; in sales we track revenue and conversion, in marketing we watch the effectiveness of campaigns relative to sales, in H.R. we work to achieve strong employee engagement and low turn-over and in operations we're always looking for more efficient ways of doing things. Those, and many other key performance indicators (KPIs), are delivered on spread sheets with numbers.

I'm convinced, though, that how we get anywhere is the result of such an intricate weaving of a multitude of factors. The numbers provide a basis but what about the conversations? What about the stories between the lines of the numbers?

More importantly, what parts of that data and those stories, and to what degree, will contribute to the "ideal" going forward?

Aha! – **"There are two worlds: the world we can measure with line and rule, and the world that we feel in our hearts and imagination."** ~ Leigh Hunt

While our business' "black box" of reports can offer a statistical history of what transpired over a given period, its ability to provide direction is limited.

Sure, if you keep doing the same thing you'll get the same results but the lesson here is in what you're measuring.

What if you added to your list of KPIs things like the number of thank-you cards you send, how many times you revisit your purpose and value statements, the frequency by which you completely unplug and recharge, the quality of your power team when you're changing directions, or your level of stress or excitement on Monday mornings? (then again, you have an "Aha" to look forward to so all Mondays are good :)) Measuring attitude, gratitude, awareness, network, clarity etc., is less common but are arguably the most igniting energy sources behind what happened before and what's to come.

Lock into your destination with all your heart, then fly, baby, fly.

Action:

How are you currently measuring results? What actions are not represented on the data that would help you get more of what you want?

_____

_____

_____

_____

_____

_____

_____

_____

_____

_____

_____

_____

_____

_____

_____

_____

_____

_____

_____

_____

I have a theory about the reason for re-gifting. See if you agree.

My theory is that people tend to buy for others things that which they themselves like as opposed to things that the other would like. They take the "Golden Rule" a little too literally.

It's not that their intentions aren't sincere – not at all – it's more that they find something that they fell in love with (or would really appreciate receiving themselves), and knowing that you are friends, they expect that you would love it, too.

Sometimes that is totally the case but often times not.

The same holds true in business.

A group of boomers will sit around the table discussing their values and in what form they like to be appreciated. The danger is in them assuming that all generations wish to be appreciated in the same way

Aha! – **"When you go fishing, you don't bring the fish food you will like, you bring food that the fish will like."** ~ Dr. Jussi Eerikäinen, Author: *Transforming Vibes, Transforming Lives!*

In a nutshell, the answer to awesome gift-giving is "empathy".

The thing is, empathy is a skill that is rare and immensely valued but extremely difficult to develop.

Why?

Because you see things through your own eyes and conditioning. You can't help but impose your thoughts and emotions on everything you see and everything you do.... gift-buying included.

In order to be empathetic you need to jump out of your own thinking and immerse yourself into someone else's – to see things through their eyes – which is an extraordinary talent.

While the basics of human nature are common amongst us all, like our need to know that we matter, recognition can be an individual thing. The secret weapon – beyond market research and focus group – is empathy.

To grow the fish in your pond, know what food they like.

Action: What questions would you ask if you were going to conduct an informal survey?

_____

_____

_____

_____

_____

_____

_____

_____

_____

_____

_____

_____

_____

_____

_____

_____

_____

_____

_____

_____

_____

_____

Did you ever have a great idea then almost immediately stop yourself in your tracks?

Maybe the idea was to call a prominent person to ask for their time, to solicit venture capital for a new model you created, gaining more twitter followers or to write your first book.

When the idea popped into your head you were enthused with what the result could mean to you; then, before you had a chance to take just one step, you called yourself off.

Why do we do that? It's like we stand in our own way!

It's actually not your fault. It's the amygdala at work; the brain structure that's responsible for autonomic responses associated with fear and fear conditioning.

It's like a "first responder". It looks for potential threats with a "safety first" attitude. It means well, protecting us from danger. The problem is, when we buy into its warnings. the little bugger can shut down our best ideas before we've had a chance to massage them.

What's worse? The more often we experience a specific fear, the stronger the distress signals! The more often we hit a wall trying to get in front of influential people, finding capital, acquiring fans or publishing, the greater the cumulative effect of "memory" and the greater the fear of trying again.

So, what's the answer? Do we allow our first response to control our course of action?

Aha! – We regret the things we don't do more than the things we do.

Your life movie should be more than your tale of survival. Perhaps your hero isn't the amygdala that is keeping you safe, but the prefrontal cortex; your rational, decision-making and more evolved area of the brain, or PC if you will. This is where the real thinking occurs. You see, you have the power to assess those fears and decide if they're real and worthy of conceit, to completely override them or anything in between. Your rational brain, your PC, is your gift of growth.

"Fear is stupid. So are regrets." ~ *Marilyn Monroe*

Action:

What might you tell yourself the next time fear is about to stop you from something you would really like to do?

_____

_____

_____

_____

_____

_____

_____

_____

_____

_____

_____

_____

_____

_____

_____

_____

_____

_____

_____

_____

_____

_____

Last week I attended a structured networking event.

Once everyone in the room introduced themselves, the moderator couldn't help but notice that people from the same company sat together... they sat together... at a networking event...

$Aha!$ – You already know the people you know.

Enriching and taking care of current relationships is always a good practice. A designated networking event, however, is a rich new playground for you to meet your next customer, or supplier, or referral partner, or hire.

Now effective networking isn't about telling your story to as many people as you can reach in the shortest period of time. Effective networking is about asking specific questions, then listening. You're listening for opportunities to help another succeed. That opportunity might come by way of your business or it might come by way of an introduction to someone else's. The important thing is this: in the bigger scheme, all efforts count.

It's comfortable for us to want to share time with people we know and like yet making new friends is easier for some than others – like me – so I think of networking events like Sesame Street for business. ☺

Absolutely, positively honor your existing relationships, and when it's time, look for awesome new ones.

Who's new in your neighbourhood?

Action:

What might you gain by looking up from your phone to connect with the person sitting beside you? (or standing in line behind you?)

It's fascinating to experience the Law of Reciprocity in action.

Sometimes the response is immediate, like smiling and having someone smile back at you. Other times is takes its own sweet time to deliver the result, like acquiring the perfect executive assistant. The Law of Reciprocity states that what we put out into the cosmos in the way of energy – thoughts, feelings, emotions – will manifest itself in physical form.

Essentially, the outcome unfolds based on what we broadcast.

I have a fear of big bodies of water.

Years ago I was encouraged to para-sail and, with fear and trepidation, I agreed and was hoisted into the air from the back of a boat. The flying part was awesome but when the boat driver decided to slow the boat to "dip" my toes into the water, the result was horrifying. As he sped up the boat in an effort to bring me back into the air, I did the opposite. I spun under water like a lure on a fishing rod, with hardly a breath. Eventually the driver stopped the boat, at which point I came to the surface, bruised and traumatized.

My fear of the water being more powerful than I, was delivered in real form. Coincidence?

Aha! – Thoughts become things.

The Law of Reciprocity is a sub-law of the Law of Vibration and interconnected with the Law of Attraction. It's precise and dependable.

The sheer knowledge that we have that kind of power – to send out intention and anticipate receiving it in true form – is really quite spectacular but knowing that we're energy beings, all part of a unified field, helps to make it make sense.

Now here's the thing: The Law makes no judgment as to what your thoughts or emotions are, it simply delivers that which you think about.

And don't think you can trick the Law by saying one thing but secretly or subconsciously expect something different. The expectation, whether it be conscious or ingrained, will win every time.

Much of our patterned thinking was established when we were too young to filter the input, which means, many of our beliefs, actions and intentions are unconsciously based on that mosaic. Now that we're all grown up, we're powerful beings, gifted with an intellect to choose our thoughts, which now means, consciously rethinking our way into favoured circumstances.

Now go ahead and wake up your luck.

Action: How does it feel to know that you have such influence over your destiny?

_____

_____

_____

_____

_____

_____

_____

_____

_____

_____

_____

_____

_____

_____

_____

_____

_____

_____

_____

_____

_____

_____

_____

_____

We can learn a lot from lobsters.

Lobsters grow by molting or shedding their shells.

Now I don't mean that they grow and then have to shed their shells, they actually grow as a result of shedding their shells.

Here's how the process works.

Before they shed their shells they grow a thin one underneath. Then they struggle out of their old shell while simultaneously absorbing water which expands their body size. They also become ravenous and eat substantially after they cast their shell and in the process, increase their size by about 20%.

So they don't grow first then molt, they grow by molting.

For a minute, think like a lobster.

What protective armour – environment, friends, attitude, food, limiting beliefs, work – are you holding on to?

Does each factor still serve your growth?

Aha! – Big growth occurs after you cast.

Often growth is somewhat invisible – like the thin new shell the lobster prepares – but once the restraint of limitation is broken, the growth is often immense and obvious.

Releasing or losing can be extremely uncomfortable. Letting go can feel like a part of you goes with it.

But it's more than okay to allow pieces to fall away and create an appetite for growth. In fact, it's crucial.

Ya, you might feel a little naked at first, but in no time you'll own new duds that'll show off all you've become... until the next time.

Action:

What's your plan for letting go of something you've outgrown that no longer serves you?

_____

_____

_____

_____

_____

_____

_____

_____

_____

_____

_____

_____

_____

_____

_____

_____

_____

_____

_____

_____

_____

_____

How often are successful people cited as being lucky?

"He was lucky because his parents had money." "She was lucky because she had natural talent." "They were lucky because…", well, fill in the blanks.

If you've ever been "lucky", and I imagine you have, then you know how it feels to be proclaimed as "lucky".

Truth is, "Luck is when preparedness meets opportunity."

In Hollywood they call it a "20-year overnight success"; they invested 20 years preparing then, one day, they stepped into the spotlight.

Oprah Winfrey, J.K Rowling, LeBron James, Henry Ford, Celine Dion, Steve Jobs, Sam Walton, Andrew Carnegie, and Michael Oher are a few of the "lucky" ones. They, too, had modest or humbling starts yet through belief and application, they rose to success.

Now, it's a common saying that opportunity only knocks once.

Is that true?

Doesn't that instill some fear that if our ship comes in, and we're at the airport, that we might miss our big opportunity?

Aha! – Opportunity is everywhere all the time!

Here's the thing. Opportunity doesn't always present itself until you're ready, or put another way, you don't see the opportunity until you've grown into it.

And the first opportunity you see might not be your opportunity anyway!

"Knowing that opportunity isn't a once-in-a-lifetime event gives you the confidence to explore your options and to keep your mind open to new opportunities. You realize that the chances have been there all along; you simply haven't seen them." ~ *Richard Carlson, Ph.D. Author: Don't Worry, Make Money.*

There are always new problems to solve, new stages being built, new partnerships being formed, new products being developed, new technologies being invented, and new markets opening up.

Your mission, should you choose to accept it, is to build your talent then, simply show up....eyes wide open, of course.

Be your own four-leaf clover.

Action:

What would you like to see come your way? How are you preparing for that opportunity?

What's your "quality quotient"? What's your ratio of high-fives to make-up calls?

We all measure this to some extent – how many times we execute flawlessly and how many times things don't go according to plan – but what is the impact of that quotient?

I know of a first-class manufacturer that processes about 1500 orders a day. For every 100 orders they process, on average, three result in complaints. Now the complaint is measured once it's filed with the resolution team so that's not counting issues that customer service handles, but for argument sake, on any given day, 45 orders go wrong. I imagine the resolutions are to redo or reroute the product or offer a discount, and while the errors can be frustrating, time-consuming and expensive, likely they're not life-threatening. Three percent says there's some work to do but it's a manageable number.

Air Canada puts about 1500 flights into the air on any given day. While there may be some delays, inconveniences and the odd bag that gets misrouted – nothing customer service can't handle – just the thought of 3% of their flights going down is unfathomable not to mention unacceptable.

Now, "quality" is very personal. Each of us defines "quality" in a different way. To some it's about education and the ability to provide creative solutions. To others it might be about response time, effective communication, order accuracy, team-oriented culture, continuous sales growth, positive customer experiences, awards and accolades, impact on society, customer loyalty or any combination. So when you divide the number of rights by wrongs – and I'll ask the question again – what is the impact of that quotient? Further, if the impact was life-altering, would that be worthy of changing behaviour?

Aha! – Act as if what you do makes a difference… because it does.

"Quality is not an act, it's a habit." ~ *Aristotle*. Aristotle, like many inspiring and noble leaders, remind us that quality does not happen randomly; it results from pure intention and deliberate action. And pure intention and deliberate action is motivated by emotions. You can't generate quality unless you're in a quality mindset.

Dr. Barbara Fredrickson, Author of "Positivity" has been studying the effect of positive emotions long before it became trendy. Her work reveals that negative emotions – fear, doubt, worry and anxiety - can close down our ability to function, while positive emotions – pride, confidence, care, love, hope, joy, interest and gratitude – will open us up to possibility.

Want to improve your quality quotient? Create a culture that breeds positive emotions.

"The simple act of caring is heroic" ~ *Edward Albert*

Action: If you were to raise the bar in one area of your life, what belief would first need to be in place?

I like a good dose of protein in the morning so I started making egg white omelets with colourful, sautéed veggies and cheese.

I thought I created the perfect breakfast until one day I sprinkled a little hot sauce on it.

Amazing that just a tiny bit of spice made such a flavourful difference.

So I decided to expand on my relationship with hot sauce and experiment with other dishes I could enhance.

Hot sauce kicked everything up a notch.

Then I started adding a little bit of my own "hot sauce" – the proverbial kind – in other areas to see what effect it might have.

I started not just "liking" people's posts but actually sharing some insights, opinions or encouragement.

I started not just accepting customers' requests but challenging them a little with some new questions to ensure we were providing the perfect solution.

I started asking people, "What are you working on?" to see if I could help in some way.

Yes, asking the question, "What would hot sauce do?" took some getting used to but the new spice is bringing enhanced value everywhere.

Comments are creating conversations, questions are generating innovation and my offer to help is frequently returned with interest in my goals.

Aha! – Hot sauce builds rapport.

You see my hot sauce usage didn't stop at my omelet, that's where it began!

A squirt here, a dash there, and my taste buds are dancing and my relationship with hot sauce is always expanding.

By adding a little proverbial hot sauce to my conversations, I've expanded on those relationships as well.

The conversation doesn't end at the "like" or the "request" or the "Nice to see you again", the conversation is actually just getting started!

Building and enhancing rapport deepens your relationships.

And let's face it: we're not companies dealing with companies, we're people dealing with people.

Relationships matter.

Put that *$&# on everything!

Action:

Which area of your life would benefit most with a sprinkling of proverbial hot sauce? What does that "hot sauce" look like?

There is always this delicate balance to our work between what needs to be done for today and what needs to be done for tomorrow.

For instance, your town council would make road construction decisions based on routing day-to-day traffic in the upset of the dig while paving the way for tomorrow's commuters.

Your wellness trainer would give you a routine that would provide you with energy today while preparing you to laugh in the face of tomorrow's aging.

The lessons you're instilling in your kids now will keep them safe today and will empower them for tomorrow's stability. So what's the split in focus and effort for today vs. tomorrow?

Many days it takes considerable effort just to keep a multitude of balls in the air where even setting aside "thinking time" about tomorrow can be too much to ask.

But here's food for thought. We've witnessed technology making a number of jobs redundant and we know the trend will inevitably continue. For instance, with the advent of self-driving cards, two to three million Americans are projected to lose their jobs in the coming decade.

Now, many great leaders suggest that the best preparation for tomorrow is to do today's work really well.

Is that advice complete? I'm wondering, where is the balance of time with school bus, truck and taxi drivers? While they're likely invested in enhancing their driving skills for today, are they in tune with the needs of tomorrow?

Aha! – **"Tomorrow belongs to those who can hear it coming"**.
~ David Bowie

Tony Robbins asks, "How am I going to live today in order to create the tomorrow I'm committed to?"

That question invites you to project yourself into the future as well as to envision what that future will actually look like!

Being exceptional at what you do by committing to mastery is only one side of the lucky penny.

The other side is to be relevant. To own both you need to be listening.

"Life is always speaking to you. First in whispers… It's subtle, those whispers. And if you don't pay attention to the whispers, it gets louder and louder. It's like getting thumped upside the head, like my grandmother used to do… You don't pay attention to that, it's like getting a brick upside your head. You don't pay attention to that, the whole brick wall falls down. Your life is speaking to you. What is it saying?"
~ *Oprah Winfrey*

Action:

Your life is speaking to you. What is it saying?

One of my favourite things to do is to brainstorm.

I love coming up with new ideas or new ways to do things.

I don't take much credit for the effort though because brainstorming for me is like channeling.

I focus on the issue then just stay open and let the ideas flow in.

Sometimes what comes out of my mouth sounds absurd and it's not uncommon that my ideas meet with resistance.

I don't mind and heck, we all need a good laugh once in a while!

The thing is, I believe brainstorming sessions shouldn't be censored as you never know what you might say that will spark an idea with someone else.

Further, you have to identify what you don't want in order to clarify what you do want.

Do you think that being timid about sharing ideas can potentially kibosh the next big breakthrough?

And ... are we doing our progress justice by casting off laughable ideas when at first appearance they don't align?

Aha! – **"Focus on the doughnut, not the hole."**
~ Vera N. Rang (my mom)

A brainstorming session is meant to take your idea or issue or project to a new level.

Therefore the focus needs to squarely be on the problem or the project.

Diverting your attention to, say, how you might feel about sharing your ideas, is actually diluting your energy and not allowing you to be totally present in building the goal.

Only when your efforts are centered on the goal are you more likely to polish a silly-sounding idea. It might be a diamond in the rough!

"It's not that I'm so smart, it's just that I stay with problems longer."
~ Albert Einstein

Be an Einstein at your next meeting… and bring the doughnuts.

Action:

Do you openly share your ideas without being attached to the response? What's the worst that can happen? What's the best?

It's a funny thing about practice.

The more we do something the better we get at it.

The more we drive our new car, the better we handle it.

The more we speak that new language, the more proficient communicators we are.

The more we lift, the more we can lift, and more easily.

When we practice something we create memory: mental memory, muscle memory and often both.

Eventually that practice becomes a habit, something we do so automatically that we barely need to think our way through it.

Creating a habit is like fueling a fire.

At first it's a lot of effort for a little spark and eventually it takes far less effort to build a blaze that takes on a life of its own.

Aha! – What you give energy to, grows.

Just like a seedling grows with nutrient soil, water and sunlight, when you give energy to an idea, a passion, a task, or a person, growth is guaranteed. It's a law of nature.

This is good news if the habit we want to create is a positive one. That repetitive, positive investment of effort pays off!

The bad news is that the same rules apply to bad habits. The more often we blow off exercise, show up late for meetings, or toss recyclable items into the trash, the easier it gets to repeat the action… unconsciously.

Sometimes building a new habit feels like you're pushing a bolder up hill. It takes deliberate, conscious, significant effort.

But if you are clear of your goal and are super excited about bringing it into reality, that emotion fuels the effort and makes it far easier.

"What you think, you become. What you feel, you attract. What you imagine, you create." ~ *Buddha*

This is the year you adopt that one new habit that'll make all the difference.

Now go kick some serious butt!!

Action:

Describe that one new habit and how good it feels to own it.

My son shared with me an earlier situation where he high-tailed it on the bus during inclement weather and a jammed schedule, to get to a watch store before their 9:00 p.m. closing. He arrived at 8:45 feeling grateful for sliding in on-time only for the shop personnel to advise they were choosing to close early and wouldn't help. They suggested he could return the next day when the store re-opened. The next day wasn't at all convenient for William and since the posted closing was 9:00 p.m., he asked for consideration and for the service he desired. The answer was still "no".

It reminded me of how often we hear "Sorry, that item is out-of-stock."

Out-of-stocks and closings are inevitable just like tides, eclipses and your phone battery dying. They can be disappointments but how they are handled is the difference between you turning away feeling unvalued OR becoming an ambassador for life. Out-of-stocks and closings actually represent instant opportunities to share your brand promise.

Here's what I mean.

If your request for inventory, for instance, is returned with a, "Sorry, that item is out of stock", the responsibility is shifted back to you to start your buying process all over again, on your own accord.

If your request for inventory is returned with a, "Sorry, that item is out of stock however I see we have more coming in next Tuesday. Can you wait? If not, we have that item in two other colours if that's a consideration. If you'd care to share why you chose this item, perhaps I can do a quick search here and see if there's something else that might work even better for you."

Aha! – **"Think long-term, day-to-day."** ~ William Mahood, Founder: VRSN

Every action – *including every inaction* – is a choice, and a reflection of your brand.

An employee wishing to close shop early might have been a necessity but the short-sighted attitude of offering an inconvenient alternative to the customer drove the customer away. And for how long? In William's case, likely forever.

While bad news is tough to deliver and difficult circumstances may cause inconvenience, they are often your best opportunity to show what you're made of.

Everyone knows life's not perfect and possibly your immediate solutions might still not be enough to solve the problem or satisfy the customer at that time.

But good effort and positive intention demonstrates that you're in it for the long haul.

It's cool to care.

Action: What would you like to hear from a customer service associate if you couldn't get what you want?

_____

_____

_____

_____

_____

_____

_____

_____

_____

_____

_____

_____

_____

_____

_____

_____

_____

_____

_____

_____

_____

_____

_____

There's a time to play it safe and there's a time to take a risk

Risk-taking can be, well, risky business.

But think about it. If no decision is a decision then isn't not taking a risk, taking a risk?

You might think you're creating vulnerability by risking change but perhaps by not changing, you may be risking being left behind

It is accepted to say that "safe" is the opposite of "risk" but by playing it safe, what are you risking?

My dad always said, "Idle hands make an idle mind". In other words if you're not experiencing you're not advancing.

And since there is no such living being that's static – you're either growing or dying – by playing it safe, you're actually shutting down.

Aha! – "Yes, risk taking is inherently failure-prone. Otherwise, it would be called sure-thing-taking". ~ Tim McMahon

A ship in harbor is safe – but that is not what ships are for. ~ *John A. Shedd, Salt from My Attic*

What's the inhibitor? "The fear of being laughed at makes cowards of us all." ~ *Mignon McLaughlin, The Neurotic's Notebook, 1960*

The truth is, "You'll always miss 100% of the shots you don't take." ~ *Wayne Gretzky*

So, "Why not go out on a limb? Isn't that where the fruit is?" ~ *Frank Scully*

Seriously, "Don't be afraid to go out on a wild goose chase; after all, that's what wild geese are for!"

Finally, "To dare is to lose one's footing momentarily. To not dare is to lose oneself". ~ *Søren Kierkegaard*

Life is worth the risk.

Action: What is your personal quote about the benefits of taking a risk?

There was a wonderful cartoon posted by golf coach Carrie Vaughan.

The cartoon showed a child expressing to his mom his reluctance in wishing to practice the violin saying, "I don't want to practice! I just want to skip ahead to the part where I'm awesome!"

Don't we all??

When my son was a junior golfer, I walked the course one day during a tournament where he wasn't playing particularly well. In fact he wanted to withdraw.

I said, "You can withdraw if you'd like – it's your tournament and your choice - but I think if you push through, you'll learn a lot more than you would on a day you're playing well."

He pushed through and played the balance of the tournament extremely well. It was what he learned about himself and his capabilities that contributed to him being an AWESOME golfer.

Aha! – **Skipping the process robs you of the lessons.**

When you can feel the greatness inside and the music wanting to come out, the exhausting effort that AWESOME takes can sometimes be stifling.

But it's the grind – the experience – that is the teacher.

In fact, I think AWESOME looks something like this:

Awareness – being fully present and aware of potential and circumstances and the choices you have around them.

Will – your internal driver, the GPS that keeps you on course.

Energy – consistent, persistent and focused energy has a cumulative effect.

Specific – there's a saying, "Practice makes perfect" but Golf Coach Sean Casey reminds you to "practice perfectly". Repetition is essential to create habits. Be specific with what you're repeating

Own – visualizing yourself already in possession of that goal puts you in the vibration of that goal. Seeing is believing.

Mentor – "You have to do it by yourself but not alone." Find someone who has achieved your goal and study with them. A good coach or mentor will inspire your personal greatness

Excited - Those big goals that will take enormous effort can be scary and exciting but if it wasn't, it wouldn't be worth your effort.

We're all born with greatness inside of us but AWESOME comes with focused experience. It really is all about the journey.

Action:

How can you get excited about practice?

My FitBit is no fashion statement but I like it. It gives me feedback on my routine and keeps me mindful of making healthy active choices.

I wasn't the first to get a FitBit. Many of my friends had one before I did and though I saw in-store displays and marketing messages for some time, I chose when to invest. Now I'm hooked; not only on my FitBit but on the company.

They have a cool on-line program that lets you sync your device with your phone or computer and not only helps you track your progress, it also rewards you with fun levels of achievement. You can also connect with your on-line friends who are FitBit enthusiasts, invested in their health.

When my FitBit died one day several months back, I went on-line, did all the recommended trouble-shooting they suggested then finally called the "help" line.

Now, if you know me you know that I put off those kinds of phone calls with <u>all</u> my might. They usually take much longer than they should, involve being transferred from one department to another or requiring supervisor's assistance, and don't always end well. With FitBit I got an intelligent person right off the bat. She easily qualified me then THANKED me for doing the trouble shooting before calling. In a matter of a few short minutes we determined that I needed a new FitBit and she offered to send me one – free of charge. It arrived the next day. Yesterday I got my "Italy" badge - apparently I have walked a distance equal to the size of Italy – and sent "challenges" to a few of my Facebook friends so we could virtually walk together.

My point is that FitBit did a fair bit of marketing before I jumped on board but it's the brand continuity between programs and people that inspire me to stay. Every aspect of their offer is consistent with their brand.

Aha! – Marketing is no longer a "department."

It's not uncommon for a marketing team to put together a kick-ass brand message and implementation program.

The test is how the message is conveyed and carried.

When there is inconsistency between the marketing message and the experience, the brand is watered-down or worse, tainted.

The essence of the brand needs to resonate with absolutely everyone in the organization and then be shared at *every* word, in *every* action, at *every* touch-point with customers, supporters, partners, teammates and stakeholders alike.

That kind of consistency is no easy task, but it's worth it.

In fact, when you make that level of consistency and satisfaction a priority, you create Brand Ambassadors – like me.

Now if you'll excuse me, I've gotta run.

Action: What would it take to find the leaks in your brand? In which areas do you wish to be most consistent?

I don't think we give ourselves enough credit.

For instance, have you ever taken on a personal trainer or an accountability buddy? If so, did you discover how many more push-ups you could do when your trainer was encouraging you, or how much longer you could hold that plank when you're competing with your buddy?

I think, on our own, we tend to undersell ourselves. Funny... we tend to have more confidence in the ability of others than we do ourselves.

Is confidence a predetermined programming or can anyone achieve confidence?

Eric Hoffer said, "If you have too little confidence, you will think you can't learn. If you have too much, you will think you don't have to learn." Either side of that spectrum is self-sabotage.

Some say confidence comes from maturity, others believe it's born of courage. Confidence is sometimes referred to as a blind faith; like we should muster confidence whether we believe ourselves or not. Then there's Robert Kiyosaki who says, "Confidence comes from discipline and training."

At what stage does confidence play a role?

Aha! – "All anything takes, really, is confidence." ~ Rachel Ward

Maybe you need to stir a little confidence into your morning coffee, then dress like you own it, smile like you deserve it, and be grateful... because you had it all along.

"You're braver than you believe, stronger than you seem, & smarter than you think." ~ *Christopher Robin as told to Pooh Bear*

And let's face it, there's nothing sexier than confidence.

Action:

What statement of encouragement would you like to see written on your bathroom mirror that you would wake up to?

_____

_____

_____

_____

_____

_____

_____

_____

_____

_____

_____

_____

_____

_____

_____

_____

_____

_____

_____

_____

_____

_____

_____

My friend, Kathy, sent me a note asking if there was such a thing as "behavioural branding" saying, "I think about this every time an employee cuts in front of me when I'm walking through a store." She continued, "Today, at the lumber yard, a new employee was whining about how her coworkers were treating her (expecting her to learn her job) instead of thanking me for being a customer as I left."

I'll bet that together we all could write quite a book about our experiences as customers! Experiences that surprised us when the actions of the employees at the business (or store, or service provider, "or hotel ...) didn't align with the brand promise.

Yes, Kathy, Behavioural Branding is a real thing.

IGI Global defines it like this: "Behavioural branding is a customer-centric strategy (that) aims to align a company's external brand promise with all employees' activities to ensure that everything that employees do is brand building, both directly and indirectly." I think Behavioural Branding is a sub-definition for "integrity" which is synonymous with "whole", "undivided", and "consistent".

Since people are the ones who convey the brand message - regardless of their hierarchical level or job description – is it fair to assume that the client relationship is dependent on word-action alignment? Do the words of the brand promise hold water if the actions aren't in harmony?

Aha! – "Don't tell me, show me." ~ M. Gabriella Morfesis

The thing about being a sensory being is that you are being influenced by messages through all of your senses simultaneously and continuously. You may see or hear the words yet but you always "experience" the message.

If someone's body language, tone, eye contact, energy or actions don't align with their words, you will know. Sometimes the actions are blatant – like a service person on their phone, not looking up, when you're standing in front of them waiting to be acknowledged – and others may be more subtle. (I once patronized a hairdresser who would talk about clients to other clients after the initial ones left the salon. The time I was in ear-shot of this conversation was the last time.)

You have to live a brand promise; in fact, everyone in the organization has to live it. Make the connection between words and actions in training; one in which ties the words that describe the brand, together with the actions that bring those words to life.

Oh, and even if you're a company of one, the same rules apply.

The accountant may say, "Cash is king", the internet marketer, "Content is king" and when it comes to branding, "Consistency is king".

Consider yourself crowned

Action:

How do you feel when someone doesn't keep their promise?

_____
_____
_____
_____
_____
_____
_____
_____
_____
_____
_____
_____
_____
_____
_____
_____
_____
_____
_____
_____
_____
_____
_____
_____
_____

Before you hire someone, do you extensively review resumes and previous performances?

Before you invest in a system, do you read testimonials from institutions similar to yours to verify a track record?

Before you begin a training program, do you verify that individuals like yourself have experienced the results you're looking for?

For some reason we've been conditioned to take a "seeing is believing" attitude.

We look for history in order to make a decision on the future.

That means we're putting faith in what has already happened to happen again.

To some extent that might offer comfort in the decision-making process but having the expectation that something will be replicated identically is making a decision facing backwards.

While the narration of the past offers record, are we suffocating our beliefs by boxing them in with only what we can see?

In order to breathe in potential, shouldn't we be closing our eyes to the past?

Aha! – Believing is seeing.

The history, whether it be an individual's skills, a system or training program all started with an idea.

There was no history; there was only a vision and belief.

In, *It's Not About the Money*, author Bob Proctor says, "The reality that you live today is the manifestation of all your past efforts. This is what has produced your present results. Your future is open to infinite possibility; it is not dependent on the past. How you think today will determine the results you achieve from this point forward – *the past has no bearing on it.*"

People, conditions and circumstances change constantly. There are no guarantees that what happened before will happen again.

What *IS* guaranteed is your imagination, which Albert Einstein says, "....is more important than knowledge".

My money is on you.

Action:

For what do you need to see proof before you believe it? In what ways would your actions change if you believed first?

_____

_____

_____

_____

_____

_____

_____

_____

_____

_____

_____

_____

_____

_____

_____

_____

_____

_____

_____

_____

_____

Innovation or complication?

Just when you get the hang of an app, a store layout or an ordering process, it changes.

And as creatures of habit, we like it when we know our way around!

So, put yourself in your customers' shoes.

What changes have you made that you swear are upgrades but may have left your customers scratching their heads?

Staying innovative is one way in which a company identifies itself.

And taking advantage of technology and trends is how we stay ahead of the curve, right?

Not so fast.

Change for internal purposes, or even to create a fresh look, is surely innovation but if that fresh approach created barriers or even steep learning curves, was it worth it?

What inspires profitable change?

$Aha!$ – "Innovation always takes the customer's point of view" ~ Michael Gerber in *The E-Myth*

The 2.0 version is welcomed when it's intuitive.

And change works intuitively better when change is quantified.

By quantifying and measuring customers' responses you can move in the direction of making it easier for your customer to do business with you.

And we all like 'easy'.

Action:

Where can you go for quality feedback when you need to make a change?

If you've ever been through the building process you know what an obstacle course a construction site can be.

Between scaffolding, temporary stairs, tarps, skids and muck, you need to be so careful where you walk and how.

If you're not paying attention it would be too easy to bump your head, scrape your arm or twist your ankle.

Wearing steel-toed shoes, safety glasses and a helmet is standard practice for that environment.

We're quite protective of our bodies - we lather on sunscreen on hot days, wear mittens in the winter, and cover our cuts with Bandaids – but how protective are we of our minds?

Our minds are as wide open and as vulnerable as our bodies yet we think nothing of exposing our minds to negativity, toxic conversations, and counter-intuitive advice.

Is it because we can't see the effects of poisonous influence or contaminated content that we allow ourselves to entertain it?

Aha! – "Safeguard your reason" ~ Epictetus

"Just as when you walk you are careful not to step on a nail or injure your foot, you should similarly take the utmost care not to in any way impair the highest faculty of your mind. "

Hand up if you're on information overload! Getting a grasp on filtering through it all and practicing "choice" takes effort at first, then it becomes a deserving habit.

Cathy Chmilnitzky, Energy Inuit and Founder of the Energy Mastery Institute, gives this advice. "Since our minds are the space within which creation is housed, we must become the Master of our Mind. To master your mind you must become an observer of your thoughts, being aware of what you're thinking at every moment. Having observed negative thinking entering the mind you can immediately replace it with a positive uplifting thought, a thought that serves your highest and best good. These higher frequency thoughts in-turn work to create a life filled with greatness."

Kind of like mittens for your mind, eh?

Action:

Understanding that habits grow from repetition, how can you protect your mind? Are there consequences when you don't?

Are your words sabotaging your best efforts?

I was in the bank today to deposit a cheque. The teller seemed fairly new so I presented the cheque, explained the currency and to which account it was intended.

She responded with, 'No problem'.

With a smiled I countered, "I hope it's not a problem!" then laughed at my comment.

I got the deer-in-the-headlights stare from her.

I replayed the conversation as she was stumped at my comment and completely unaware of her auto-responder – "no problem" – which, by the way, she continued to use as we interacted further.

Two observations:

In an effort to be courteous, she, in reality, was associating me with potentially being a problem.

Because her response was automatic, repeating "no problem" was becoming ingrained in her work attitude.

(Remember that the mind doesn't compute a negative so if you focus on getting out of debt, for instance, what your mind actually sees is "debt", not the fact that you want to get out of it. You need to focus on "abundance.")

Now, what was that credo again? That customers are not an interruption to our work, they're the reason for our work?

So if we joyfully serve but our words are subliminally contrary, are we undermining our best intentions?

Aha! – "Think twice before you speak, because your words and influence will plant the seed of either success or failure in the mind of another" ~ Napoleon Hill

Like you, I'm a big believer that actions speak louder than words – and my teller really was delightful and efficient – however we can't ignore the impact words have on our emotions and those of others.

And make no mistake: our self talk is equally as important as the words we share out loud.

Choose your words. Choose your world.

Action: What is your auto-responder to a frequently asked question? Is it really what you mean to say?

Think of the last time you went to see a speaker, a trainer or sat in on an education session. What was the topic? What was your take-away?

The educator or facilitator likely delivered information that, if you employ it, will change your course dramatically. But also likely is that the magnitude of the impact of the material was directly related to the teacher's ability to relate the material to you.

I could tell you that I ran 10k which, without a frame of reference – to say that 10k is 6 miles or 24 times around a quarter-mile track or, for me, 53 minutes of running – you might not be able to relate to what 10k means. I could say that my FitBit lasts a long time but "long" is, also, relative. When I relate that it will last four to five days, you're onside with my description of "long."

Same holds true for your marketing message.

Saying that your car goes from zero-100km in 7.3 seconds or that you offer the best in service or that you carry all the name brands from Italy just creates more questions.

How can we help our customers instantly grasp our value?

Aha! – Start with what's familiar.

The disconnect between companies and customers might very well be in the relatable portion of the brand message. You and your audience absolutely, positively have to be on the same page.

There are a few ways to relate:

- Using similes: making a comparison using the words "like" or "as". For example, "The lightning lit up the sky like fireworks", or, "The eclipse made the day sky as dark as night".
- Speaking metaphorically: making a comparison using a figure of speech or citing something that relates to what you're describing. "Her daughter's room was a disaster area.", and "To me, new networking events are a sea of nameless faces." give you a glimpse.
- Telling stories: giving a real-life example of how you will enhance your customer's world

You know that suicide for any business is trying to be all things to all people. Be laser-sharp with your focus then develop a story or a sentence that perfectly describes you in a way that relates.

"Breakfast of Champions." "Think different". "Inspiring Results on Purpose"

Sometimes a few choice words are all you need!

Action: Write a few words or a short sentence that describes your personal brand in a way in which anyone can relate.

We're experiencing one angry planet.

"Devastating", "levelling", "catastrophic", "once-in-a-lifetime", "powerful", "deadly" are some of the descriptors for nature's lashings. From fire to flood and everything in between, there is hardly a soul not connected, in some way, to the earth's unsettled nature.

The connection might be your crawling escape on the interstate, waiting in a shelter to go home, the inability to get in contact with a friend or loved one caught in a disaster zone, or simply the emotional impact of watching, online or on T.V., thousands upon thousands of people – just like you – whose lives are being tried by a shift in the earth, wind-lashing, rising water or uncontrollable fire.

Everyone responds differently to disaster. Some question the karmic response, others look at second-hand impact (like rising gas or food prices), and some feel helpless or hopeless or both. There can be an isolation factor that accompanies loss, and subsequent unwelcome change.

How do we make sense of challenges and get through devastating loss and change?

Aha! – Grieve. Gratitude. Grow.

Grieve – it's important to acknowledge when things don't go as you had hoped, planned or expected. Seeing the impact for what and releasing yourself from feeling victimized, frees you of destructive and counter-productive emotion.

Gratitude – in all disastrous situations, heroes emerge. In some form of rescue – emotionally, physically, or financially – help arrives; not always from where you expect but always for which you will be profoundly grateful

Grow – in the midst of disaster you won't see a rainbow. Only when the "storm" passes, and you take control of that which you can and accept the wisdom and support of others, will the new order reveal itself.

Whether it's your corporation, your health, your home, your family, or any other part of life, you can only take care of it to the extent that you can take care of it. The Universe is an intricate weave of energy and information that, despite your best intentions, also has influence over you.

Understand that sometimes bad things happen to good people.

Be grateful for what IS going right.

Grow as you should.

Know that it's all part of your story

Action: In which area have you ever felt victimized? How can you re-frame that to grow stronger as a result of the circumstance or experience?

With cold and flu season approaching, the advice about the causes and cures will also be circulating in abundance.

We're bound to hear "Don't go outside with wet hair." "Eat chicken soup." and "Get lots of vitamin C." on more than one occasion.

There is no shortage of opinions or theories about protecting yourself of these contagious little bugs.

If we didn't dry our hair after swim class then came down with the sniffles, we might equate that combination to what brought us down.

But is that really the case or just a coincidence?

Whether or not the story is true, we might accept it if it makes sense or aligns with what we've experienced in the past.

We adopt these kinds of stories in so many aspects of our lives on a daily basis.

The ones like, "He didn't return my email so that must mean they gave the business to someone else." OR "She didn't call me on my birthday so she must be mad at me." How about, "He didn't clean up the dishes because he's a slob.", OR "That car cut me off because she's such a poor driver."

Sound familiar?

Preconceived conclusions may bring acceptance to a situation but are we being fair to ourselves by creating our own ending?

Can making an assumption throw us down the wrong path?

$\mathcal{A}ha!$ – "The object of the superior man is truth" ~ Confucius

Maybe he didn't return your email because he was on holidays.

Perhaps she didn't call you on your birthday because she lost power in the storm.

Maybe he didn't do the dishes because his sister's plane arrived early and he chose to bolt to the airport.

Perhaps the car cut you off because the driver was trying to get a choking child to the hospital.

Misinformation can cause stress and stress plays havoc on your immune system and a weak immune system makes you more susceptible to catching the common cold.

Protect your mind and your body. Know the truth, like that chicken soup really does lessen cold symptoms and make you feel better.

To your health!

Action: What are the ramifications of imposing your conditioned views on assumptions?

_____
_____
_____
_____
_____
_____
_____
_____
_____
_____
_____
_____
_____
_____
_____
_____
_____
_____
_____
_____
_____
_____

Do you participate in spring cleaning?

In Canada, when everything is covered in a white blanket and the chilly air required layers of protective clothing, we hold "spring" in our minds as our incentive to push through knowing that "spring" never disappoints.

It rains a little more at that time of year but, coupled with the added daylight, nature is clearly encouraging life to blossom. The fresh, aromatic air is filled with negative ions generated from the rain. It's so energizing and all the more reason to open our windows. And when we do, we're treated to the sounds of children giggling as they toss the ball, play tag and climb the monkey bars. Sometimes those sounds are drowned out by leaf-blowers, lawn mowers and power-washers but they're all welcome signs that spring is in the air.

At this season change, everyone arises from hibernation to begin to de-clutter, give everything a good scrub, get organized, and welcome back outdoor living. It's somewhat of a seasonal ritual that feels so good!

Jonathan Fader, Ph.D. writes in *Psychology Today*, "While spring cleaning has the obvious benefits of an organized closet, a sparkling counter top, and possibly more open spaces, more importantly, it has been associated with improved mood, decreased stress and heightened creativity."

With that in mind, should the inspiration that "spring" represents need only be seasonal?

Aha! – Make spring a habit.

When you're overwhelmed with toppling piles and disorganized spaces, these distractions are likely adding to your stress level. Cleaning, sorting and organizing can be time-consuming but the psychological benefits of an efficient, productive environment are well worth it.

Spring is invigorating. Spring is inspiring. Spring tends to lift your spirits, fill you with hope, open your eyes to new possibilities with renewed energy, and breathe imaginative life into your dreams and aspirations. So, anytime you want to get your "creative" on, think spring!

"Spring is nature's way of saying, let's party!" ~ *Robin Williams*

Action:

Identify a physical spot in your environment that is blocking your creativity because of its clutter. What order would be created in your mind as a result of creating order in that physical space?

ABOUT THE AUTHOR

Originally from St. Catharines, Ontario – in the heart of the Niagara wine region – Jae M. Rang has enjoyed a life-long passion for peak performance and self-development.

At the age of just 16, Jae got her pilot's license – before she even had her driver's license! Then, as a professional figure skater, she performed with the Ice Follies, and spent fifteen years teaching both figure- and power-skating.

And now, as Founder and Chief Inspiring Officer of the promotional marketing firm JAE associates Ltd., Jae is a leader in the field of influencing behavioral change through sensory media.

With training under Bob Proctor, and certified as a speaker with Life Success Productions, Jae also gives talks and conducts workshops across North America on two of her favorite topics (and areas of major expertise) – Promotional Marketing and Personal Development. Yet she still considers herself an eternal and insatiable student of human behavior… which Jae says really took off with the birth of her son, William.

A VERY proud Canadian and avid sports fan, Jae ALWAYS stands for the playing of the National Anthem… even when watching a hockey game in her own living room! And when she's not working with clients, teaching, studying, writing, or being "the best Mom I can be"… Jae is most likely working on her golf game.

Jae is also the best-selling author of **SENSORY MEDIA, Discover the Way to Anchor Your Brand and Be Memorable**, and **50 Simple Ways to Increase Brand Visibility**. And her weekly "Aha Moments" column is enjoyed by thousands of readers in more than a dozen countries.

Succeed deliberately!
www.ahamoments.ca

Made in the USA
San Bernardino, CA
10 December 2017